A COMMON WORD

A COMMON WORD
Text and Reflections

A RESOURCE FOR PARISHES AND MOSQUES

Edited by Lejla Demiri

MUSLIM ACADEMIC TRUST

First published 2011 by
The Muslim Academic Trust
14 St Paul's Road
Cambridge CB1 2EZ
United Kingdom

© This collection the Muslim Academic Trust, 2011

Distributed by Central Books Ltd
www.centralbooks.co.uk

ISBN 978 1 902350 07 3

English calligraphy by Adam Williamson
Printed in Turkey by Mega Basım

CONTENTS

FOREWORD

He has ordained the same religion for you
as that which He commended to Noah,
and that which We revealed to you,
and that which We commended to Abraham
and Moses and Jesus,
that you steadfastly uphold the religion, and be
not divided therein.

(Qur'an 42:13)

SINCE ITS LAUNCH on 13 October 2007, *A Common Word between Us and You*, the open letter from Muslim religious leaders to the Christian churches, has become the leading initiative in interfaith dialogue between Christians and Muslims in today's globalised world. The letter was initially signed and supported by 138 prominent Muslim scholars, clerics and intellectuals, representing all significant denominations and schools of thought in Islam. The list includes names of outstanding individuals such as Grand Mufti Ali Jum'a of Egypt, Sheikh Abd Allah bin Bayyah of Mauritania, Sheikh Sa'id Ramadan al-Buti of Syria, Grand Mufti Mustafa Cerić of Bosnia, Sheikh Habib Ali al-Jifri and Sheikh Habib Umar of Yemen, Professors Seyyed Hossein Nasr and Ingrid Mattson, Imam Yahya Sergio Yahé Pallavicini, and many others. Since its launch, the document has been endorsed by hundreds of other Islamic leaders, scholars and organizations, as well as by thousands of ordinary Muslims.

The *Common Word* document is a genuine effort to recognise the common ground between the two Abrahamic traditions, Islam and Christianity, on the basis of the two foundational principles which they share: love of God and love of neighbour.[1] It invites Christians to join hands with Muslims to promote world peace and harmony in the name of God. It calls on all the heirs of the Abrahamic heritage to promote true dialogue in the spirit of mutual understanding and respect, as inspired by the Qur'anic message:

> *Say: O People of the Scripture! Come to a common word between us and you: that we shall worship none but God, and that we shall ascribe no partner unto Him, and that none of us shall take others for lords beside God. And if they turn away, then say: Bear witness that we are they who have surrendered (unto Him).* (Q 3:64)

Building on a set of citations from Muslim and Christian scriptures, the document celebrates the values both faiths share, while acknowledging their differences.

The socio-historical context of the *Common Word* suggests that the principle of love is intertwined with the core values of mercy and compassion. The letter opens '*In the Name of God, the Compassionate, the Merciful*', thereby invok-

---

1 That neighbour (*jar*) in the Islamic conception includes non-Muslim neighbours is stressed by, for instance, Abu Hamid al-Ghazali, *Ihya' Ulum al-Din* (Cairo: al-Halabi, AH 1347), II, 188 (*Huquq al-jiwar*); see also Ibn Rajab al-Hanbali, *The Compendium of Knowledge and Wisdom*, trans. Abdassamad Clarke (London: Turath Publishing, 1428/2007), p.224. The parallels and differences between Muslim and Christian notions of 'neighbour' are worth exploring, yet this would go beyond the scope of the present volume.

ing God's blessings and support in accordance with the tradition Muslims follow in every possible action they take. Moreover, the *Common Word* was issued on the occasion of the Eid al-Fitr festival of 1428/2007, celebrating the completion of Ramadan, the month of exceptional divine mercy and compassion, during which, Muslims believe, the Qur'an was revealed. Deeply rooted in the divine message conveyed by the scriptures, the *Common Word* endeavours to be faithful to the prophetic tradition of mercy and love, and to the Divine love which is prior to our creation and any of our acts.[2] What is more, its launch marks the first anniversary of the 'Open Letter to the Pope' (13 October 2006), when 38 Muslim religious authorities and scholars from around the world sent their joint response to Pope Benedict XVI one month after his address in Regensburg (13 September 2006). Not only do the *Common Word* and the 'Open Letter to the Pope' represent a genuine intellectual openness and readiness to tackle various misconceptions that identify Islam with unrepresentative extremes today, but more importantly they also testify to the strong desire on the part of Muslims to build bridges as witnesses to a scriptural tradi-

---

2 For mainstream Islamic thought, God's love for man, and man's love for God, are not self-interested or laden with preconditions, although clearly God does not love sinners as much as He loves those who work to heal His creation; see for instance Muhammad Sa'id Ramadan al-Buti, *al-Hubb fi'l-Qur'an wa-dawr al-hubb fi hayat al-insan* (Damascus: Dar al-Fikr, 2009); Eric Ormsby, *Ghazali: the Revival of Islam* (Oxford: Oneworld, 2008), p.138. An alternative to Ghazali's perspective is present in the 'hardline' thinkers of the minority Hanbali school, such as Ibn Taymiyya, who hold that love for God is akin to loving a benefactor (see Joseph Norment Bell, *Love Theory in Later Hanbalite Islam* [Albany: State University of New York Press, 1979]). For a more popular treatment see Mahnaz Heydarpoor, *Love in Christianity and Islam: a Contribution to Religious Ethics* (London: New City, 2002), 61-3 (chapter on 'God's Love as the Highest Reason for Creation'), and p.67 on God's love for wrongdoers.

tion which upholds and promotes peaceful coexistence with other faith communities.

Much has been accomplished since the document's launch. Its official website[3] now includes a roll-call of the leading Christian figures of different denominations who have warmly and positively responded to the open letter. It includes Pope Benedict XVI, the late Russian Orthodox Patriarch Alexei II, the Archbishop of Canterbury Dr. Rowan Williams, the Presiding Bishop of the Lutheran World Federation Bishop Mark Hanson, the President and General Secretary of the World Alliance of Reform Churches, the President of the World Baptist Alliance, the President of the World Council of Churches, the Council of Bishops of Methodist Churches, the Head of the World Evangelical Alliance, the Mennonite Church, Quaker leaders and a number of other Orthodox and Eastern Orthodox Patriarchs, Catholic cardinals, archbishops, heads of national churches, deans of theological seminaries, well-known preachers, professors and leading Christian scholars of Islam. Among these many initiatives an *Open Letter* signed by over three hundred leading US Evangelical and 'mainline' leaders and scholars is regarded as one of the most remarkable Christian responses to the *Common Word*. The letter, which bore the title 'Loving God and Neighbour Together' was written and coordinated by Professor Miroslav Volf of the Yale Divinity School, and was published as a full-page spread in the *New York Times* in November 2007.

In addition to institutional and individual responses, four major international conferences have taken place since the publication of the *Common Word*. In July 2008, the first major *Common Word* conference was held at Yale University, followed by a second conference at the University of Cam-

3 www.acommonword.com

bridge in October 2008, co-hosted by Cambridge University, the Royal Aal al-Bayt Institute for Islamic Thought, and the Archbishop of Canterbury. In November 2008, the first International Catholic-Muslim Forum, hosted by Pope Benedict XVI, took place at the Vatican, and was addressed by the Pope himself; while in October 2009 Georgetown University and the Prince Al-Waleed Bin Talal Center for Muslim-Christian Understanding, in partnership with the Royal Aal al-Bayt Institute for Islamic Thought, held a fourth major conference which focused on some of the initiative's practical and diplomatic entailments.

Over the past three years, the *Common Word* has also given rise to a growing number of other international and local symposiums, lectures, workshops, conferences and other interfaith activities all over the world. Various academic books and journals have already been dedicated to the *Common Word,* and a number of MA and MPhil. dissertations (e.g. at Harvard University, the Theological Seminary at the University of Tübingen and the Centre for the Study of Islam in Birmingham) have focused on it. Besides a growing interest in academic circles, a range of local and grassroots-level Christian-Muslim initiatives based on the *Common Word* have appeared in countries such as India, Pakistan, Bangladesh, Canada, South Africa, the USA, and the UK.[4]

The *Common Word* initiative bore further fruit when, on October 20, 2010, the UN General Assembly unanimously approved the designation of the first week in February of every year to be a 'World Interfaith Harmony Week'. Based substantially on the *Common Word* document, but with reference also to the *Common Ground* initiative (a separate

---

4 For a detailed account of the *Common Word's* accomplishments, see http://acommonword.com/en/a-common-word/2-general/161-qa-common-wordq-accomplishments-2007-2009.html.

venture by many of the same Muslim scholars which aimed to further communication and reconciliation with the global Buddhist community),[5] the resolution incorporated a major interfaith event into the UN's calendar for the first time. Stressing its purely voluntary nature, and that everyone who wished to mark it should do so 'according to their own religious traditions or convictions', the resolution, and the speech by Prince Ghazi bin Muhammad of Jordan, who presented it to the General Assembly, acknowledged that the phrase 'Love of God and the Neighbour', or 'Love of the Good and Love of Neighbour', will necessarily be interpreted in divergent ways, and that no attempt at syncretism or reductionism was being made.

The current volume, which seeks to place the *Common Word* in the hands of a wide spectrum of mosque and church communities, includes two scholarly yet accessible contributions to the *Common Word* initiative, authored by two outstanding academics: David Burrell C.S.C., one of the most prominent Catholic scholars of Islam, who is the Hesburgh Professor of Theology and Philosophy at the University of Notre Dame, Indiana, and Tim Winter (Abdal Hakim Murad), a leading Muslim scholar from the University of Cambridge, dean of the Cambridge Muslim College and one of the first signatories of the *Common Word*, who has significantly contributed to this project since the document was first drafted.

Burrell's article, 'Christians and Muslims Breathe a New Spirit,' is based on a lecture he presented at the Catholic Chaplaincy, University of Cambridge on February 20, 2009. He begins with a short analysis of Pope Benedict XVI's Regensburg address, demonstrating a genuinely

---

5 See Reza Shah-Kazemi, HH the Dalai Lama, and others, *Common Ground between Islam and Buddhism* (Louisville KY: Fons Vitae, 2010).

critical and open perspective concerning what was a controversial event. This is followed by a discussion of the significance and ultimate goal of interfaith dialogue which, in Burrell's view, should attend to 'meaning' rather than to 'truth'. In other words, dialogue should be 'a means ... of stating what we believe,' and giving 'witness to what we have received from God' as holders of scriptural traditions. By examining three theological examples: the Christian doctrine of the Trinity, intradivine relations (*personae*) and original sin, which he identifies as 'neuralgic issues,' Burrell seeks to demonstrate how 'interfaith exchange can now offer an apt vehicle for developing doctrine,' for traditions are 'relative to one another in ways that can prove mutually fruitful rather than isolating.' He ultimately arrives at the conclusion that 'interfaith comparative inquiry' helps the members of each tradition to appreciate, as well as to witness the divine revelation they have received. As an example of a fruitful dialogue, his approach brings us back to the importance of what the *Common Word* has to offer to the contemporary theological discourse between Muslims and Christians.

Murad's paper, 'Human Dignity and Mutual Respect,' was one of the two keynote Muslim addresses given at the First Catholic-Muslim Forum at the Vatican in 2008.[6] His main emphasis is on the importance of what Christianity and Islam as two Abrahamic faiths have to offer to resolve the spiritual crisis of modernity as experienced in the currently 'Godless society' of Europe. As he rightly points out, Muslim-Christian cooperation and mutual respect are vitally needed in the campaign against pessimism and relativism, as embodied in 'Europe's lack of faith, and the diminu-

---

6 The other was given by the Iranian thinker Professor Seyyed Hossein Nasr.

tion of human dignity and conviviality.' It is through the common ideal of the dignity and honour of humanity that members of these two faiths should stand in solidarity with one another in overcoming the postmodern crisis which affects the faithful of both traditions. Yet this cooperation and mutual support should not remain merely pragmatic; rather they must entail a theological conversation. The institution of the family, Israeli-Palestinian conflict and other crises and tragedies around the world (such as Darfur, Eastern Zaire and elsewhere) where human dignity is being outraged, and also natural disasters and global famine, are identified as the most important areas where the Muslim-Christian commitment to human dignity can find practical expression. This is required, as Murad concludes, by the Abrahamic principle of submission to God's will and a readiness to sacrifice unsparingly, a perspective Muslims and Christians share in their respective traditions.

Both papers agree on the perfect timeliness of the *Common Word*, in an age when mutual respect and cooperation between the believers of Islam and Christianity is becoming increasingly vital. This is not the first time, however, that members of our respective traditions have come together to converse. Historical accounts of social, intellectual and theological encounters go as far back as the earliest days of Islam. In particular, we recall the poignant examples of Waraqa b. Nawfal, the Christian cousin of the Prophet's wife Khadija, who identified Muhammad as a prophet in the Biblical tradition; the scripture-based conversations which took place between a Christian king of Abyssinia and a group of early Muslim refugees who found shelter and friendly protection under his rule; theological discussions with the Christian delegation of Najran, who were welcomed to worship and pray at the Prophet's mosque in Medina, and many others. It comes as no surprise to see such

encounters in great profusion among subsequent genera-
tions when, as a recent study points out, for more than four
hundred years (7th – 11th centuries), some fifty percent
of the world's Christians lived in the midst of Muslims.[7]
European history is not isolated from such interactions ei-
ther. Since Islam's arrival in Spain in the 8th century and its
subsequent advance into the Balkans and Eastern Europe in
the 14th century, Muslims and Christians, despite certain
inevitable difficulties and tensions, found themselves not
only living together, but also sharing a common culture in
architecture, poetry, literature, music and scholarship.

The *Common Word*, grounded as it is in scriptural tradition and Abrahamic commitment to generosity and
self-giving, is an inspiring reminder of all the principles we share. In addition to empowering us to challenge
the myth of the so-called 'clash of civilizations', which
sets Islam and the West as eternal and hopeless adversar-
ies, it encourages us to stand united for the sake of world
peace and harmony, despite the voices that describe religion as one of the paradigms of conflict. So in this spirit, let us celebrate our shared ideals and commitment to
the well-being of humanity by heeding Rumi's words,
'We are God's family and need His milk, *Creation is a
family in God*'.[8]

Dr Lejla Demiri

RAMADAN 1431, AUGUST 2010,
CAMBRIDGE

---

7 Sydney H. Griffith, *The Church in the Shadow of the Mosque: Christians
and Muslims in the World of Islam* (Princeton-Oxford: Princeton University Press, 2008), p. 11.
8 Rumi, *Spiritual Verses: The First Book of the Masnavi-ye Ma'navi*, trans.
Alan Williams, London: Penguin Books, 2006, p. 91.

On the occasion of the *Eid al-Fitr al-Mubarak* 1428 A.H. / October 13th 2007 C.E., and on the one year anniversary of the Open Letter of 38 Muslim Scholars to H.H. Pope Benedict XVI,

An Open Letter and Call from Muslim Religious Leaders to:

His Holiness Pope Benedict XVI,

His All-Holiness Bartholomew I, Patriarch of Constantinople, New Rome,

His Beatitude Theodoros II, Pope and Patriarch of Alexandria and All Africa,

His Beatitude Ignatius IV, Patriarch of Antioch and All the East,

His Beatitude Theophilos III, Patriarch of the Holy City of Jerusalem,

His Beatitude Alexy II, Patriarch of Moscow and All Russia,

His Beatitude Pavle, Patriarch of Belgrade and Serbia,

His Beatitude Daniel, Patriarch of Romania,

His Beatitude Maxim, Patriarch of Bulgaria,

His Beatitude Ilia II, Archbishop of Mtskheta-Tbilisi, Catholicos-Patriarch of All Georgia,

His Beatitude Chrisostomos, Archbishop of Cyprus,

His Beatitude Christodoulos, Archbishop of Athens and All Greece,

His Beatitude Sawa, Metropolitan of Warsaw
and All Poland,

His Beatitude Anastasios, Archbishop of Tirana, Durrës and
All Albania,

His Beatitude Christoforos, Metropolitan of the Czech and
Slovak Republics,

His Holiness Pope Shenouda III, Pope of Alexandria and Patriarch
of All Africa on the Apostolic Throne of St. Mark,

His Beatitude Karekin II, Supreme Patriarch and Catholicos of
All Armenians,

His Beatitude Ignatius Zakka I, Patriarch of Antioch and All the East,
Supreme Head of the Universal Syrian Orthodox Church,

His Holiness Mar Thoma Didymos I, Catholicos of the East on the
Apostolic Throne of St. Thomas and the Malankara Metropolitan,

His Holiness Abune Paulos, Fifth Patriarch and Catholicos of Ethiopia,
Tekle Haymanot, Archbishop of Axum,

His Beatitude Mar Dinkha IV, Patriarch of the Holy Apostolic Catholic
Assyrian Church of the East,

The Most Rev. Rowan Williams, Archbishop of Canterbury,

Rev. Mark S. Hanson, Presiding Bishop of the Evangelical Lutheran
Church in America, and President of the Lutheran World Federation,

Rev. George H. Freeman, General Secretary,
World Methodist Council,

Rev. David Coffey, President of the Baptist World Alliance,

Rev. Setri Nyomi, General Secretary of the World Alliance of
Reformed Churches,

Rev. Dr. Samuel Kobia, General Secretary,
World Council of Churches,

And Leaders of Christian Churches, everywhere …

A Common Word between Us and You
(Summary and Abridgement)

MUSLIMS AND CHRISTIANS together make up well over half of the world's population. Without peace and justice between these two religious communities, there can be no meaningful peace in the world. The future of the world depends on peace between Muslims and Christians.

The basis for this peace and understanding already exists. It is part of the very foundational principles of both faiths: love of the One God, and love of the neighbour. These principles are found over and over again in the sacred texts of Islam and Christianity. The Unity of God, the necessity of love for Him, and the necessity of love of the neighbour is thus the common ground between Islam and Christianity. The following are only a few examples:

Of God's Unity, God says in the Holy Qur'an: *Say: He is God, the One! / God, the Self-Sufficient Besought of all!* (Al-Ikhlas, 112:1-2). Of the necessity of love for God, God says in the Holy Qur'an: *So invoke the Name of thy Lord and devote thyself to Him with a complete devotion* (Al-Muzzammil, 73:8). Of the necessity of love for the neighbour, the Prophet

Muhammad ﷺ said: "*None of you has faith until you love for your neighbour what you love for yourself.*"

In the New Testament, Jesus Christ ﷺ said: '*Hear, O Israel, the Lord our God, the Lord is One. / And you shall love the Lord your God with all your heart, with all your soul, with all your mind, and with all your strength.* ' *This is the first commandment. / And the second, like it, is this:* '*You shall love your neighbour as yourself.* ' *There is no other commandment greater than these.*"

(Mark 12:29-31)

In the Holy Qur'an, God Most High enjoins Muslims to issue the following call to Christians (and Jews—the *People of the Scripture*):

> *Say: O People of the Scripture! Come to a common word between us and you: that we shall worship none but God, and that we shall ascribe no partner unto Him, and that none of us shall take others for lords beside God. And if they turn away, then say: Bear witness that we are they who have surrendered (unto Him).* (Aal 'Imran 3:64)

The words: *we shall ascribe no partner unto Him* relate to the Unity of God, and the words: *worship none but God*, relate to being totally devoted to God. Hence they all relate to the *First and Greatest Commandment*. According to one of the oldest and most authoritative commentaries on the Holy Qur'an the words: *that none of us shall take others for lords beside God*, mean 'that none of us should obey the other in disobedience to what God has commanded'. This relates to the Second Commandment because justice and freedom of religion are a crucial part of love of the neighbour.

Thus in obedience to the Holy Qur'an, we as Muslims invite Christians to come together with us on the basis of what is common to us, which is also what is most essential to our faith and practice: the *Two Commandments* of love.

IN THE NAME OF GOD, THE COMPASSIONATE, THE
MERCIFUL, AND MAY PEACE AND BLESSINGS BE
UPON THE PROPHET MUHAMMAD

A COMMON WORD BETWEEN US AND YOU

In the Name of God, the Compassionate, the Merciful,
"Call unto the way of thy Lord with wisdom and fair exhortation,
and contend with them in the fairest way. Lo! thy Lord is Best Aware
of him who strayeth from His way, and He is Best Aware of
those who go aright."

(The Holy Qur'an, Al-Nahl, 16:125)

(I)
LOVE OF GOD

LOVE OF GOD IN ISLAM

The Testimonies of Faith

THE CENTRAL CREED of Islam consists of the two testimonies of faith or *Shahadahs*[i], which state that: *There is no god but God, Muhammad is the messenger of God*. These Two Testimonies are the *sine qua non* of Islam. He or she who testifies to them is a Muslim; he or she who denies them is not a Muslim. Moreover, the Prophet Muhammad ﷺ said: *The best remembrance is: 'There is no god but God'*....[ii]

The Best that all the Prophets have said

Expanding on *the best remembrance*, the Prophet Muhammad ﷺ also said:

> *The best that I have said—myself, and the prophets that came before me—is: 'There is no god but God, He Alone, He hath no associate, His is the sovereignty and His is the praise and He hath power over all things'* [iii]

The phrases which follow the First Testimony of faith are all from the Holy Qur'an; each describe a mode of love of God, and devotion to Him.

The words: *He Alone*, remind Muslims that their hearts[iv] must be devoted to God Alone, since God says in the Holy Qur'an: *God hath not assigned unto any man two hearts within his body* (Al-Ahzab, 33:4). God is Absolute and therefore devotion to Him must be totally sincere.

The words: *He hath no associate*, remind Muslims that they must love God uniquely, without rivals within their souls, since God says in the Holy Qur'an: *Yet there are men who take rivals unto God: they love them as they should love God. But those of faith are more intense in their love for God* ... (Al-Baqarah, 2:165). Indeed, *[T]heir flesh and their hearts soften unto the remembrance of God* ... (Al-Zumar, 39:23).

The words: *His is the sovereignty*, remind Muslims that their minds or their understandings must be totally devoted to God, for *the sovereignty* is precisely everything in creation or existence and everything that the mind can know. And all is in God's Hand, since God says in the Holy Qur'an: *Blessed is He in Whose Hand is the sovereignty, and, He is Able to do all things* (Al-Mulk, 67:1).

The words: *His is the praise* remind Muslims that they must be grateful to God and trust Him with all their sentiments and emotions. God says in the Holy Qur'an:

And if thou wert to ask them: Who created the heavens and the earth, and constrained the sun and the moon (to their appointed work)? they would say: God. How then are they turned away? God maketh the provision wide for whom He will of His servants, and straiteneth it for whom (He will). Lo! God is Aware of all things. And if thou wert to ask them: Who causeth water to come down from the sky, and therewith

reviveth the earth after its death? they verily would say: God.
Say: Praise be to God! But most of them have no sense.
(Al-'Ankabut, 29:61-63)[v]

For all these bounties and more, human beings must always be truly grateful:

> *God is He Who created the heavens and the earth, and causeth*
> *water to descend from the sky, thereby producing fruits as food*
> *for you, and maketh the ships to be of service unto you, that*
> *they may run upon the sea at His command, and hath made*
> *of service unto you the rivers; And maketh the sun and the*
> *moon, constant in their courses, to be of service unto you, and*
> *hath made of service unto you the night and the day. And*
> *He giveth you of all ye ask of Him, and if ye would count*
> *the graces of God ye cannot reckon them. Lo! man is verily a*
> *wrong-doer, an ingrate.* (Ibrahim, 14:32-34)[vi]

Indeed, the *Fatihah*—which is the *greatest chapter in the Holy Qur'an*[vii]—starts with praise to God:

> *In the Name of God, the Infinitely Good, the All-Merciful.*
> *Praise be to God, the Lord of the worlds.*
> *The Infinitely Good, the All-Merciful.*
> *Owner of the Day of Judgement.*
> *Thee we worship, and Thee we ask for help.*
> *Guide us upon the straight path.*
> *The path of those on whom is Thy Grace, not those who*
> *deserve anger nor those who are astray.* (Al-Fatihah, 1:1-7)

The *Fatihah*, recited at least seventeen times daily by Muslims in the canonical prayers, reminds us of the praise and gratitude due to God for His Attributes of Infinite

Goodness and All-Mercifulness, not merely for His Goodness and Mercy to us in this life but ultimately, on the Day of Judgement[viii] when it matters the most and when we hope to be forgiven for our sins. It thus ends with prayers for grace and guidance, so that we might attain—through what begins with praise and gratitude—salvation and *love*, for God says in the Holy Qur'an: *Lo! those who believe and do good works, the Infinitely Good will appoint for them love.* (Maryam, 19:96)

The words: *and He hath power over all things*, remind Muslims that they must be mindful of God's Omnipotence and thus fear God[ix]. God says in the Holy Qur'an:

> ... *[A]nd fear God, and know that God is with the God-fearing. Spend your wealth for the cause of God, and be not cast by your own hands to ruin; and do good. Lo! God loveth the virtuous.....*
>
> (Al-Baqarah, 2:194-5)

> *[A]nd fear God, and know that God is severe in punishment.*
> (Al-Baqarah, 2:196)

Through fear of God, the actions, might and strength of Muslims should be totally devoted to God. God says in the Holy Qur'an:

> ... *[A]nd know that God is with those who fear Him.*
> (Al-Tawbah, 9:36)

> *O ye who believe! What aileth you that when it is said unto you: Go forth in the way of God, ye are bowed down to the ground with heaviness. Take ye pleasure in the life of the world rather than in the Hereafter? The comfort of the life of*

the world is but little in the Hereafter. If ye go not forth He will afflict you with a painful doom, and will choose instead of you a folk other than you. Ye cannot harm Him at all. God is Able to do all things.

(Al-Tawbah, 9:38-39)

☾

The words: *His is the sovereignty and His is the praise and He hath power over all things*, when taken all together, remind Muslims that just as everything in creation glorifies God, everything that is in their souls must be devoted to God:

All that is in the heavens and all that is in the earth glorifieth God; His is the sovereignty and His is the praise and He hath power over all things. (Al-Taghabun, 64:1)

For indeed, all that is in people's souls is known, and accountable, to God:

He knoweth all that is in the heavens and the earth, and He knoweth what ye conceal and what ye publish. And God is Aware of what is in the breasts (of men).

(Al-Taghabun, 64:4)

As we can see from all the passages quoted above, souls are depicted in the Holy Qur'an as having three main faculties: the mind or the intelligence, which is made for comprehending the truth; the will which is made for freedom of choice, and sentiment which is made for loving the good and the beautiful.[x] Put in another way, we could say that man's soul knows through *understanding* the truth, through *willing* the good, and through virtuous emotions and *feeling* love for God. Continuing in the same chapter of the Holy Qur'an (as that quoted above), God orders people to fear Him as much as possible, and to listen (and thus to understand the truth); to obey (and thus to will the good), and to spend (and thus to exercise love and virtue), which, He says, is better for our souls. By engaging *everything* in our souls—the faculties of knowledge, will, and love—we may come to be purified and attain ultimate success:

So fear God as best ye can, and listen, and obey, and spend; that is better for your souls. And those who are saved from the pettiness of their own souls, such are the successful.

(Al-Taghabun, 64:16)

(

In summary then, when the entire phrase *He Alone, He hath no associate, His is the sovereignty and His is the praise and He hath power over all things* is added to the testimony of faith—*There is no god but God*—it reminds Muslims that their hearts, their individual souls and all the faculties and powers of their souls (or simply their *entire* hearts and souls) must be totally devoted and attached to God. Thus God says to the Prophet Muhammad ﷺ in the Holy Qur'an:

Say: Lo! my worship and my sacrifice and my living and my dying are for God, Lord of the Worlds. He hath no partner. This am I commanded, and I am first of those who surrender (unto Him). Say: Shall I seek another than God for Lord, when He is Lord of all things? Each soul earneth only on its own account, nor doth any laden bear another's load...

(Al-An'am, 6:162-164)

These verses epitomize the Prophet Muhammad's ﷺ complete and utter devotion to God. Thus in the Holy Qur'an God enjoins Muslims who truly love God to follow this example,[xi] in order in turn to be loved[xii] by God:

6

Say, (O Muhammad, to mankind): If ye love God, follow me; God will love you and forgive you your sins. God is Forgiving, Merciful

(Aal 'Imran, 3:31)

Love of God in Islam is thus part of complete and total devotion to God; it is not a mere fleeting, partial emotion. As seen above, God commands in the Holy Qur'an: *Say: Lo! my worship and my sacrifice and my living and my dying are for God, Lord of the Worlds. He hath no partner.* The call to be totally devoted and attached to God heart and soul, far from being a call for a mere emotion or for a mood, is in fact an injunction requiring all-embracing, constant and active love of God. It demands a love in which the innermost spiritual heart and the whole of the soul—with its intelligence, will and feeling—participate through devotion.

(

None Comes with Anything Better

We have seen how the blessed phrase: *There is no god but God, He Alone, He hath no associate, His is the sovereignty and His is the praise and He hath power over all things*—which is the best that all the prophets have said—makes explicit what is implicit in *the best remembrance* (*There is no god but God*) by showing what it requires and entails, by way of devotion. It remains to be said that this blessed formula is also in itself a sacred invocation—a kind of extension of the First Testimony of faith (*There is no god but God*)—the ritual repetition of which can bring about, through God's grace, some of the devotional attitudes it demands, namely, loving and being devoted to God with all one's heart, all one's soul, all one's mind, all one's will or strength, and all one's sentiment. Hence the Prophet Muhammad commended this remembrance by saying:

> *He who says: 'There is no god but God, He Alone, He hath no associate, His is the sovereignty and His is the praise and He hath power over all things' one hundred times in a day, it is for them equal to setting ten slaves free, and one hundred good deeds are written for them and one hundred bad deeds are effaced, and it is for them a protection from the devil for that day until the evening. And none offers anything better than that, save one who does more than that.*[xiii]

In other words, the blessed remembrance, *There is no god but God, He Alone, He hath no associate, His is the sovereignty and His is the praise and He hath power over all things*, not only requires and implies that Muslims must be totally devoted to God and love Him with their whole hearts and their whole souls and all that is in them, but provides a way, like its beginning (the testimony of faith)—through its frequent repetition[xiv]—for them to realize this love with everything they are.

God says in one of the very first revelations in the Holy Qur'an: *So invoke the Name of thy Lord and devote thyself to Him with a complete devotion* (Al-Muzzammil, 73:8).

❧

LOVE OF GOD AS THE *FIRST AND GREATEST* COMMANDMENT IN THE BIBLE

The *Shema* in the Book of Deuteronomy (6:4-5), a centrepiece of the Old Testament and of Jewish liturgy, says:

Hear, O Israel: The LORD our God, the LORD is one!
You shall love the LORD your God with all your heart, and
with all your soul, and with all your strength.[xv]

Likewise, in the New Testament, when Jesus Christ, the Messiah ❦, is asked about the Greatest Commandment, he answers ❦:

But when the Pharisees heard that he had silenced the Sad-
ducees, they gathered together. Then one of them, a lawyer,
asked Him a question, testing Him, and saying, "Teacher,
which is the great commandment in the law?" Jesus said to
him, "'You shall love the LORD your God with all your
heart, with all your soul, and with all your mind.' This is
the first and greatest commandment. And the second is like
it: 'You shall love your neighbour as yourself.' On these two
commandments hang all the Law and the Prophets."

(Matthew 22:34-40)

And also:

Then one of the scribes came, and having heard them
reasoning together, perceiving that he had answered them well,
asked him, "Which is the first commandment of all?" Jesus
answered him, "The first of all the commandments is: 'Hear,
O Israel, the LORD our God, the LORD is one. And you
shall love the LORD your God with all your heart, with all
your soul, with all your mind, and with all your strength.'
This is the first commandment. And the second, like it, is this:
'You shall love your neighbour as yourself.' There is no other
commandment greater than these."

(Mark 12:28-31)

The commandment to love God fully is thus the *First and Greatest Commandment* of the Bible. Indeed, it is to be found in a number of other places throughout the Bible including:

Deuteronomy 4:29, 10:12, 11:13 (also part of the *Shema*), 13:3, 26:16, 30:2, 30:6, 30:10; Joshua 22:5; Mark 12:32-33 and Luke 10:27-28.

However, in various places throughout the Bible, it occurs in slightly different forms and versions. For instance, in Matthew 22:37 (*You shall love the LORD your God with all your heart, with all your soul, and with all your mind*), the Greek word for "heart" is *kardia*, the word for "soul" is *psyche*, and the word for "mind" is *dianoia*. In the version from Mark 12:30 (*And you shall love the LORD your God with all your heart, with all your soul, with all your mind, and with all your strength*) the word "strength" is added to the aforementioned three, translating the Greek word *ischus*.

The words of the lawyer in Luke 10:27 (which are confirmed by Jesus Christ ﷺ in Luke 10:28) contain the same four terms as Mark 12:30. The words of the scribe in Mark 12:32 (which are approved of by Jesus Christ ﷺ in Mark 12:34) contain the three terms *kardia* ("heart"), *dianoia* ("mind"), and *ischus* ("strength").

In the *Shema* of Deuteronomy 6:4-5 (*Hear, O Israel: The LORD our God, the LORD is one! You shall love the LORD your God with all your heart, and with all your soul, and with all your strength*). In Hebrew the word for "heart" is *lev*, the word for "soul" is *nefesh*, and the word for "strength" is *me'od*.

In Joshua 22:5, the Israelites are commanded by Joshua ﷺ to love God and be devoted to Him as follows:

> "*But take careful heed to do the commandment and the law which Moses the servant of the LORD commanded you, to love the LORD your God, to walk in all His ways, to keep His commandments, to hold fast to Him, and to serve Him with all your heart and with all your soul.*" (Joshua 22:5)

What all these versions thus have in common—despite the language differences between the Hebrew Old Testament, the original words of Jesus Christ ﵇ in Aramaic, and the actual transmitted Greek of the New Testament—is the command to love God fully with one's heart and soul and to be fully devoted to Him. This is the First and Greatest Commandment for human beings.

In the light of what we have seen to be necessarily implied and evoked by the Prophet Muhammad's ﷺ blessed saying: '*The best that I have said—myself, and the prophets that came before me—is: 'There is no god but God, He Alone, He hath no associate, His is the sovereignty and His is the praise and He hath power over all things,'*[xvi] we can now perhaps understand the words '*The best that I have said—myself, and the prophets that came before me*' as equating the blessed formula *'There is no god but God, He Alone, He hath no associate, His is the sovereignty and His is the praise and He hath power over all things'* precisely with the 'First and Greatest Commandment' to love God, with all one's heart and soul, as found in various places in the Bible. That is to say, in other words, that the Prophet Muhammad ﷺ was perhaps, through inspiration, restating and alluding to the Bible's First Commandment. God knows best, but certainly we have seen their effective similarity in meaning. Moreover, we also do know (as can be seen in the endnotes), that both formulas have another remarkable parallel: the way they arise in a number of slightly differing versions and forms in different contexts, all of which, nevertheless, emphasize the primacy of total love and devotion to God.[xvii]

LOVE OF THE NEIGHBOUR

LOVE OF THE NEIGHBOUR IN ISLAM

THERE ARE NUMEROUS injunctions in Islam about the necessity and paramount importance of love for—and mercy towards—the neighbour. Love of the neighbour is an essential and integral part of faith in God and love of God because in Islam without love of the neighbour there is no true faith in God and no righteousness. The Prophet Muhammad 鷺 said:

> "*None of you has faith until you love for your brother what you love for yourself.*"[xviii]

And: "*None of you has faith until you love for your neighbour what you love for yourself.*"[xix]

However, empathy and sympathy for the neighbour—and even formal prayers— are not enough. They must be accompanied by generosity and self-sacrifice. God says in the Holy Qur'an:

> *It is not righteousness that ye turn your faces*[xx] *to the East and the West; but righteous is he who believeth in God and the Last Day and the angels and the Scripture and the prophets; and giveth wealth, for love of Him, to kinsfolk and to orphans and the needy and the wayfarer and to those who ask, and to set slaves free; and observeth proper worship and payeth the poor-due. And those who keep their treaty when they make one, and the patient in tribulation and adversity and time of stress. Such are they who are sincere. Such are the pious.*
>
> (Al-Baqarah 2:177)

And also:

> *Ye will not attain unto righteousness until ye expend of that which ye love. And whatsoever ye expend, God is Aware thereof.*
>
> (Aal 'Imran, 3:92)

Without giving the neighbour what we ourselves love, we do not truly love God or the neighbour.

LOVE OF THE NEIGHBOUR IN THE BIBLE

We have already cited the words of the Messiah, Jesus Christ ☙, about the paramount importance, second only to the love of God, of the love of the neighbour:

> *This is the first and greatest commandment. And the second is like it: 'You shall love your neighbour as yourself.' On these two commandments hang all the Law and the Prophets.*
>
> (Matthew 22:38-40)

And:

> *And the second, like it, is this: 'You shall love your neighbour as yourself.' There is no other commandment greater than these.*

> (Mark 12:31)

It remains only to be noted that this commandment is also to be found in the Old Testament:

> *You shall not hate your brother in your heart. You shall surely rebuke your neighbour, and not bear sin because of him. You shall not take vengeance, nor bear any grudge against the children of your people, but you shall love your neighbour as yourself: I am the LORD.* (Leviticus 19:17-18)

Thus the Second Commandment, like the First Commandment, demands generosity and self-sacrifice, and *On these two commandments hang all the Law and the Prophets.*

(III)

COME TO A COMMON WORD BETWEEN US AND YOU

A COMMON WORD

WHILST ISLAM AND Christianity are obviously different religions—and whilst there is no minimising some of their formal differences—it is clear that the *Two Greatest Commandments* are an area of **common ground** and a link between the Qur'an, the Torah and the New Testament. What prefaces the Two Commandments in the Torah and the New Testament, and what they arise out of, is the Unity of God—that there is only one God. For the *Shema* in the Torah, starts: (Deuteronomy 6:4) *Hear, O Israel: The LORD our God, the LORD is one!* Likewise, Jesus ﷺ said: (Mark 12:29) *"The first of all the commandments is: 'Hear, O Israel, the LORD our God, the LORD is one".* Likewise, God says in the Holy Qur'an: *Say: He, God, is One. God, the Self-Sufficient Besought of all.* (*Al-Ikhlas*, 112:1-2). Thus the Unity of God, love of Him, and love of the neighbour form a common ground upon which Islam and Christianity (and Judaism) are founded.

This could not be otherwise since Jesus ﷺ said (Matthew 22:40): *"On these two commandments hang all the Law and the Prophets."* Moreover, God confirms in the Holy Qur'an that the Prophet Muhammad ﷺ brought nothing fundamentally or essentially new: *Naught is said to thee (Muhammad) but what already was said to the messengers before thee (Fussilat 41:43).* And: *Say (Muhammad): I am no new thing among the messengers (of God), nor know I what will be done with me or with you. I do but follow that which is Revealed to me, and I am but a plain warner (Al-Ahqaf, 46:9).* Thus also God in the Holy Qur'an confirms that the same eternal truths of the Unity of God, of the necessity for total love and devotion to God (and thus shunning false gods), and of the necessity for love of fellow human beings (and thus justice), underlie all true religion:

And verily We have raised in every nation a messenger, (proclaiming): Worship God and shun false gods. Then some of them (there were) whom God guided, and some of them (there were) upon whom error had just hold. Do but travel in the land and see the nature of the consequence for the deniers!
(Al-Nahl, 16:36)

We verily sent Our messengers with clear proofs, and revealed with them the Scripture and the Balance, that mankind may stand forth in justice ....

(Al-Hadid, 57:25)

Come to a Common Word!

In the Holy Qur'an, God Most High tells Muslims to issue the following call to Christians (and Jews—the *People of the Scripture*):

> *Say: O People of the Scripture! Come to a common word between us and you: that we shall worship none but God, and that we shall ascribe no partner unto Him, and that none of us shall take others for lords beside God. And if they turn away, then say: Bear witness that we are they who have surrendered (unto Him).*

(Aal 'Imran 3:64)

Clearly, the blessed words: *we shall ascribe no partner unto Him* relate to the Unity of God. Clearly also, worshipping *none but God*, relates to being totally devoted to God and hence to the *First and Greatest Commandment*. According to one of the oldest and most authoritative commentaries (*tafsir*) on the Holy Qur'an—the *Jami' Al-Bayan fi Ta'wil Al-Qur'an* of Abu Ja'far Muhammad bin Jarir Al-Tabari (d. 310 A.H. 923 C.E.)—*that none of us shall take others for lords beside God*, means 'that none of us should obey in disobedience to what God has commanded, nor glorify them by prostrating to them in the same way as they prostrate to God'. In other words, that Muslims, Christians and Jews should be free to each follow what God commanded them, and not have 'to prostrate before kings and the like'[xxi]; for God says elsewhere in the Holy Qur'an: *Let there be no compulsion in religion ... (Al-Baqarah, 2:256)*. This clearly relates to the Second Commandment and to love of the neighbour of which justice[xxii] and freedom of religion are a crucial part. God says in the Holy Qur'an:

God forbiddeth you not those who warred not against you on account of religion and drove you not out from your homes, that ye should show them kindness and deal justly with them. Lo! God loveth the just dealers. (Al-Mumtahinah, 60:8)

We thus as Muslims invite Christians to remember Jesus's words in the Gospel (Mark 12:29-31):

... the LORD our God, the LORD is one. And you shall love the LORD your God with all your heart, with all your soul, with all your mind, and with all your strength.' This is the first commandment. And the second, like it, is this: 'You shall love your neighbour as yourself.' There is no other commandment greater than these.

As Muslims, we say to Christians that we are not against them and that Islam is not against them—so long as they do not wage war against Muslims on account of their religion, oppress them and drive them out of their homes, (in accordance with the verse of the Holy Qur'an [Al-Mumtahinah, 60:8] quoted above). Moreover, God says in the Holy Qur'an:

They are not all alike. Of the People of the Scripture there is a staunch community who recite the revelations of God in the night season, falling prostrate (before Him). They believe in God and the Last Day, and enjoin right conduct and forbid indecency, and vie one with another in good works. These are of the righteous. And whatever good they do, nothing will be rejected of them. God is Aware of those who ward off (evil).
(Aal-'Imran, 3:113-115)

Is Christianity necessarily against Muslims? In the Gospel Jesus Christ ﷺ says:

> He who is not with me is against me, and he who does not gather with me scatters abroad. (Matthew 12:30)

> For he who is not against us is on our side. (Mark 9:40)

> ... for he who is not against us is on our side. (Luke 9:50)

According to the *Blessed Theophylact's*[xxiii] *Explanation of the New Testament*, these statements are not contradictions because the first statement (in the actual Greek text of the New Testament) refers to demons, whereas the second and third statements refer to people who recognised Jesus ﷺ, but were not Christians. Muslims recognize Jesus Christ ﷺ as the Messiah, not in the same way Christians do (but Christians themselves anyway have never all agreed with each other on Jesus Christ's ﷺ nature), but in the following way: ... *the Messiah Jesus son of Mary is a Messenger of God and His Word which he cast unto Mary and a Spirit from Him ...* (Al-Nisa', 4:171). We therefore invite Christians to consider Muslims *not against* and thus *with them*, in accordance with Jesus Christ's ﷺ words here.

Finally, as Muslims, and in obedience to the Holy Qur'an, we ask Christians to come together with us on the common essentials of our two religions ... *that we shall worship none but God, and that we shall ascribe no partner unto Him, and that none of us shall take others for lords beside God ...* (Aal 'Imran, 3:64).

Let this common ground be the basis of all future interfaith dialogue between us, for our common ground is that on which hangs *all the Law and the Prophets* (Matthew 22:40). God says in the Holy Qur'an:

Say (O Muslims): We believe in God and that which is revealed unto us and that which was revealed unto Abraham, and Ishmael, and Isaac, and Jacob, and the tribes, and that which Moses and Jesus received, and that which the prophets received from their Lord. We make no distinction between any of them, and unto Him we have surrendered. And if they believe in the like of that which ye believe, then are they rightly guided. But if they turn away, then are they in schism, and God will suffice thee against them. He is the Hearer, the Knower. (Al-Baqarah, 2:136-137)

Between Us and You

Finding common ground between Muslims and Christians is not simply a matter for polite ecumenical dialogue between selected religious leaders. Christianity and Islam are the largest and second largest religions in the world and in history. Christians and Muslims reportedly make up over a third and over a fifth of humanity respectively. Together they make up more than 55% of the world's population, making the relationship between these two religious communities the most important factor in contributing to meaningful peace around the world. If Muslims and Christians are not at peace, the world cannot be at peace. With the terrible weaponry of the modern world; with Muslims and Christians intertwined everywhere as never before, no side can unilaterally win a conflict between more than half of the world's inhabitants. Thus our common future is at stake. The very survival of the world itself is perhaps at stake.

And to those who nevertheless relish conflict and destruction for their own sake or reckon that ultimately they stand to gain through them, we say that our very eternal souls are all also at stake if we fail to sincerely make every effort to make peace and come together in harmony. God says in the Holy Qur'an:

Lo! God enjoineth justice and kindness, and giving to kinsfolk, and forbiddeth lewdness and abomination and wickedness. He exhorteth you in order that ye may take heed.
(Al Nahl, 16:90).

Jesus Christ ﷺ said:

Blessed are the peacemakers … (Matthew 5:9),

and also:

For what profit is it to a man if he gains the whole world and loses his soul? (Matthew 16:26).

So let our differences not cause hatred and strife between us. Let us vie with each other only in righteousness and good works. Let us respect each other, be fair, just and kind to another and live in sincere peace, harmony and mutual goodwill. God says in the Holy Qur'an:

And unto thee have We revealed the Scripture with the truth, confirming whatever Scripture was before it, and a watcher over it. So judge between them by that which God hath revealed, and follow not their desires away from the truth which hath come unto thee. For each We have appointed a law and a way. Had God willed He could have made you one community. But that He may try you by that which He hath given you (He hath made you as ye are). So vie one with another in good works. Unto God ye will all return, and He will then inform you of that wherein ye differ.

(Al-Ma'idah, 5:48)

Wal-Salaamu 'Alaykum,
Pax Vobiscum.

NOTES

i In Arabic: *La illaha illa Allah Muhammad rasul Allah*. The two *Shahadah*s actually both occur (albeit separately) as phrases in the Holy Qur'an (in *Muhammad* 47:19, and *Al-Fath* 48:29, respectively).

ii *Sunan Al-Tirmidhi, Kitab Al-Da'awat*, 462/5, no. 3383; *Sunan Ibn Majah*, 1249/2.

iii *Sunan Al-Tirmidhi, Kitab Al-Da'awat, Bab al-Du'a fi Yawm 'Arafah, Hadith* no. 3934.
 It is important to note that the additional phrases, *He Alone, He hath no associate, His is the sovereignty and His is the praise and He hath power over all things*, all come from the Holy Qur'an, in exactly those forms, albeit in different passages. *He Alone*—referring to God—is found at least six times in the Holy Qur'an (7:70; 14:40; 39:45; 40:12; 40:84 and 60:4). *He hath no associate*, is found in exactly that form at least once (*Al-An'am*, 6:173). *His is the sovereignty and His is the praise and He hath power over all things*, is found in exactly this form once in the Holy Qur'an (*Al-Taghabun*, 64:1), and parts of it are found a number of other times (for instance, the words, *He hath power over all things*, are found at least five times: 5:120; 11:4; 30:50; 42:9 and 57:2).

iv   **The Heart.**
In Islam the (spiritual, not physical) heart is the organ of perception of spiritual and metaphysical knowledge. Of one of the Prophet Muhammad's ﷺ greatest visions God says in the Holy Qur'an: *The inner heart lied not (in seeing) what it saw. (al-Najm*, 53:11) Indeed, elsewhere in the Holy Qur'an, God says: *[F]or indeed it is not the eyes that grow blind, but it is the hearts, which are within the bosoms, that grow blind. (Al-Hajj*, 22:46; see whole verse and also: 2:9-10; 2:74; 8:24; 26:88-89; 48:4; 83:14 et al.. There are in fact over a hundred mentions of the heart and its synonyms in the Holy Qur'an.)

23

Now there are different understandings amongst Muslims as regards the direct Vision of God (as opposed to spiritual realities as such) God, be it in this life or the next—God says in the Holy Qur'an (of the Day of Judgement):

> That day will faces be resplendent, Looking toward their Lord; (Al-Qiyamah, 75:22-23)

Yet God also says in the Holy Qur'an:

> Such is God, your Lord. There is no God save Him, the Creator of all things, so worship Him. And He taketh care of all things. Vision comprehendeth Him not, but He comprehendeth (all) vision. He is the Subtle, the Aware. Proofs have come unto you from your Lord, so whoso seeth, it is for his own good, and whoso is blind is blind to his own hurt. And I am not a keeper over you. (Al-An'am, 6:102-104)

Howbeit, it is evident that the Muslim conception of the (spiritual) heart is not very different from the Christian conception of the (spiritual) heart, as seen in Jesus's ﷺ words in the New Testament: *Blessed are the pure in heart, for they shall see God.* (Matthew 5:8); and Paul's words: *For now we see in a mirror, dimly, but then face to face. Now I know in part, but then I shall know just as I am known.* (1 Corinthians 13:12)

v See also: *Luqman*, 31:25.

vi See also: *Al-Nahl*, 16:3-18.

vii *Sahih Bukhari, Kitab Tafsir Al-Qur'an, Bab ma Ja'a fi Fatihat Al-Kitab* (*Hadith* no.1); also: *Sahih Bukhari, Kitab Fada'il Al-Qur'an, Bab Fadl Fatihat Al-Kitab*, (*Hadith* no.9), no. 5006.

viii The Prophet Muhammad ﷺ said:

> God has one hundred mercies. He has sent down one of them between genii and human beings and beasts and animals and because of it they feel with each other; and through it they have mercy on each other; and through it, the wild animal feels for its offspring. And God has delayed ninety-nine mercies through which he will have mercy on his servants on the Day of Judgement. (*Sahih Muslim, Kitab Al-Tawbah*; 2109/4; no. 2752; see also *Sahih Bukhari, Kitab Al-Riqaq*, no. 6469).

ix **Fear of God is the Beginning of Wisdom.**

The Prophet Muhammad ﷺ is reported to have said: *The chief part of wisdom is fear of God—be He exalted* (*Musnad al-Shihab*, 100/1; Al-Daylami, *Musnad Al-Firdaws*, 270/2; Al-Tirmidhi, *Nawadir Al-Usul*; 84/3; Al-Bayhaqi, *Al-Dala'il* and Al-Bayhaqi, *Al-Shu'ab*; Ibn Lal, *Al-Makarim*; Al-Ash'ari,

Al-Amthal, et al.) This evidently is similar to the Prophet Solomon's ﷺ words in the Bible: The *fear of the LORD is the beginning of Wisdom* .... (Proverbs 9:10); and: *The fear of the LORD is the beginning of knowledge.* (Proverbs 1:7)

x **The Intelligence, the Will and Sentiment in the Holy Qur'an.**
Thus God in the Holy Qur'an tells human being to believe in Him and call on Him (thereby using the intelligence) with fear (which motivates the will) and with hope (and thus with sentiment):

> *Only those believe in Our revelations who, when they are reminded of them, fall down prostrate and hymn the praise of their Lord, and they are not scornful, / Who forsake their beds to cry unto their Lord in fear and hope, and spend of that We have bestowed on them. No soul knoweth what is kept hid for them of joy, as a reward for what they used to do.* (Al-Sajdah, 32:15-17)

> *(O mankind!) Call upon your Lord humbly and in secret. Lo! He loveth not aggressors. Work not confusion in the earth after the fair ordering (thereof), and call on Him in fear and hope. Lo! the mercy of God is near unto the virtuous.* (Al-A'raf, 7:55-56)

Likewise, the Prophet Muhammad ﷺ himself is described in terms which manifest knowledge (and hence the intelligence), eliciting hope (and hence sentiment) and instilling fear (and hence motivating the will):

> *O Prophet! Lo! We have sent thee as a witness and a bringer of good tidings and a warner.* (Al-Ahzab, 33:45)

> *Lo! We have sent thee (O Muhammad) as a witness and a bearer of good tidings and a warner,* (Al-Fath, 48:8)

xi   *A Goodly Example.*
The love and total devotion of the Prophet Muhammad ﷺ to God is for Muslims the model that they seek to imitate. God says in the Holy Qur'an:

> *Verily in the messenger of God ye have a goodly example for him who hopeth for God and the Last Day, and remembereth God much.*
>
> (Al-Ahzab, 33:21)

The totality of this love excludes worldliness and egotism, and is itself beautiful and loveable to Muslims. Love of God is itself loveable to Muslims. God says in the Holy Qur'an:

> *And know that the messenger of God is among you. If he were to obey you in many matters, ye would surely fall into misfortune; but God hath made*

*the faith loveable to you and hath beautified it in your hearts, and hath made
disbelief and lewdness and rebellion hateful unto you. Such are they who are
the rightly guided. (Al-Hujurat, 49:7)*

xii This 'particular love' is in addition to God's universal Mercy *which
embraceth all things (Al-A'raf, 7:156)*; but God knows best.

xiii *Sahih Al-Bukhari, Kitab Bad' al-Khalq, Bab Sifat Iblis wa Junudihi;
Hadith no. 3329.*

OTHER VERSIONS OF THE BLESSED SAYING

This blessed saying of the Prophet Muhammad's ﷺ is found in dozens
of *hadith* (sayings of the Prophet Muhammad ﷺ in differing contexts in
slightly varying versions.

The one we have quoted throughout in the text (*There is no god but
God, He alone. He hath no associate. His is the sovereignty, and His is the praise,
and He hath power over all things*) is in fact the shortest version. It is to be
found in *Sahih al-Bukhari: Kitab al-Adhan* (no. 852); *Kitab al-Tahajjud* (no.
1163); *Kitab al-'Umrah* (no. 1825); *Kitab Bad' al-Khalq* (no. 3329); *Kitab
al-Da'awat* (nos. 6404, 6458, 6477); *Kitab al-Riqaq* (no. 6551); *Kitab al-
I'tisam bi'l-Kitab* (no. 7378); in *Sahih Muslim: Kitab al-Masajid* (nos. 1366,
1368, 1370, 1371, 1380); *Kitab al-Hajj* (nos. 3009, 3343); *Kitab al-Dhikr
wa'l-Du'a'* (nos. 7018, 7020, 7082, 7084); in *Sunan Abu Dawud: Kitab al-
Witr* (nos. 1506, 1507, 1508); *Kitab al-Jihad* (no. 2772); *Kitab al-Kharaj* (no.
2989); *Kitab al-Adab* (nos. 5062, 5073, 5079); in *Sunan al-Tirmidhi: Kitab
al-Hajj* (no. 965); *Kitab al-Da'awat* (nos. 3718, 3743, 3984); in *Sunan al-
Nasa'i: Kitab al-Sahw* (nos. 1347, 1348, 1349, 1350, 1351); *Kitab Manasik
al-Hajj* (nos. 2985, 2997); *Kitab al-Iman wa'l-Nudhur* (no. 3793); in *Sunan
Ibn Majah: Kitab al-Adab* (no. 3930); *Kitab al-Du'a'* (nos. 4000, 4011); and
in *Muwatta' Malik: Kitab al-Qur'an* (nos. 492, 494); *Kitab al-Hajj* (no. 831).

A longer version including the words *yuhyi wa yumit*—(There is no
god but God, He alone. He hath no associate. His is the sovereignty, and
His is the praise. He giveth life, and He giveth death, and He hath power
over all things.)—is to be found in *Sunan Abu Dawud: Kitab al-Manasik*
(no. 1907); in *Sunan al-Tirmidhi: Kitab al-Salah* (no. 300); *Kitab al-Da'awat*
(nos. 3804, 3811, 3877, 3901); and in *Sunan al-Nasa'i: Kitab Manasik al-Hajj*
(nos. 2974, 2987, 2998); *Sunan Ibn Majah: Kitab al-Manasik* (no. 3190).

Another longer version including the words *bi yadihi al-khayr*—
(There is no god but God, He alone. He hath no associate. His is the
sovereignty, and His is the praise. In His Hand is the good, and He hath
power over all things.)—is to be found in *Sunan Ibn Majah: Kitab al-Adab*
(no. 3931); *Kitab al-Du'a'* (no. 3994).

The longest version, which includes the words *yuhyi wa yumit wa Huwa Hayyun la yamut bi yadihi al-khayr*—(*There is no god but God, He alone. He hath no associate. His is the sovereignty, and His is the praise. He giveth life, and He giveth death. He is the Living, who dieth not. In His Hand is the good, and He hath power over all things*)—is to be found in *Sunan al-Tirmidhi*: *Kitab al-Da'awat* (no. 3756) and in *Sunan Ibn Majah*: *Kitab al-Tijarat* (no. 2320), with the difference that this latter *hadith* reads: *bi yadihi al-khayr kuluhu* (in His Hand is *all* good).

It is important to note, however, that the Prophet Muhammad ﷺ, only described the first (shortest) version as: *the best that I have said— myself, and the prophets that came before me*, and only of that version did the Prophet ﷺ say: *And none comes with anything better than that, save one who does more than that.*

(These citations refer to the numbering system of *The Sunna Project's Encyclopaedia of Hadith* (*Jam' Jawami' al-Ahadith wa'l-Asanid*), prepared in cooperation with the scholars of al-Azhar, which includes *Sahih al-Bukhari, Sahih Muslim, Sunan Abu Dawud, Sunan al-Tirmidhi, Sunan al-Nasa'i, Sunan Ibn Majah*, and *Muwatta' Malik*.)

xiv   Frequent Remembrance of God in the Holy Qur'an.

The Holy Qur'an is full of injunctions to invoke or remember God frequently:

> *Remember the name of thy Lord at morn and evening.* (*Al-Insan*, 76:25)

> *So remember God, standing, sitting and [lying] down on your sides*
> (*Al-Nisa*, 4:103).

> *And do thou (O Muhammad) remember thy Lord within thyself humbly and with awe, below thy breath, at morn and evening. And be not thou of the neglectful* (*Al-A'raf*, 7:205).

> *... Remember thy Lord much, and praise (Him) in the early hours of night and morning* (*Aal 'Imran*, 3:41).

> *O ye who believe! Remember God with much remembrance. And glorify Him early and late* (*Al-Ahzab*, 33:41-42).

(See also: 2:198-200; 2:203; 2:238-239; 3:190-191; 6:91; 7:55; 7:180; 8:45; 17:110; 22:27-41; 24:35-38; 26:227; 62:9-10; 87:1-17, et al.)

Similarly, the Holy Qur'an is full of verses that emphasize the paramount importance of the Remembrance of God (see: 2:151-7; 5:4;

6:118; 7:201; 8:2-4; 13:26-28; 14:24-27; 20:14; 20:33-34; 24:1; 29:45; 33:35; 35:10; 39:9; 50:37; 51:55-58; and 33:2; 39:22-23 and 73:8-9 as already quoted, et al.), and the dire consequences of not practising it (see: 2:114; 4:142; 7:179-180; 18:28; 18:100-101; 20:99-101; 20:124-127; 25:18; 25:29; 43:36; 53:29; 58:19; 63:9; 72:17 et al.; see also 107:4-6). Hence God ultimately says in the Holy Qur'an:

> *Has not the time arrived for the believers that their hearts in all humility should engage in the remembrance of God .... ? (Al-Hadid, 57:16);*

> *.... [S]lacken not in remembrance of Me (Taha, 20:42), and:*

> *Remember your Lord whenever you forget (Al-Kahf, 18:24).*

xv Herein all Biblical Scripture is taken from the New King James Version. Copyright © 1982 by Thomas Nelson Inc. Used by permission. All rights reserved.

xvi Sunan *Al-Tirmithi, Kitab Al-Da'awat, Bab al-Du'a fi Yawm 'Arafah, Hadith* no. 3934. *Op. cit..*

xvii   ***In the Best Stature***
Christianity and Islam have comparable conceptions of man being created in the best stature and from God's own breath. The Book of Genesis says:

> (Genesis, 1:27) *So God created man in His own image; in the image of God He created him; male and female He created them.*

And:

> (Genesis, 2:7) *And the LORD God formed man of the dust of the ground, and breathed into his nostrils the breath of life; and man became a living being.*

And the Prophet Muhammad ﷺ said: *Verily God created Adam in His own image.* (*Sahih Al-Bukhari, Kitab Al-Isti'than,* 1; *Sahih Muslim, Kitab Al-Birr* 115; *Musnad Ibn Hanbal,* 2: 244, 251, 315, 323 etc. et al.)

> *And We created you, then fashioned you, then told the angels: Fall ye prostrate before Adam! And they fell prostrate, all save Iblis, who was not of those who make prostration. (Al-A'raf, 7:11)*

> *By the fig and the olive By Mount Sinai, And by this land made safe Surely We created man of the best stature Then We reduced him to the lowest of the low, Save those who believe and do good works, and theirs is a reward unfailing. So who henceforth will give the lie to the about the judgment? Is not God the wisest of all judges? (Al-Tin, 95:1-8)*

God it is Who appointed for you the earth for a dwelling-place and the sky for a canopy, and fashioned you and perfected your shapes, and hath provided you with good things. Such is God, your Lord. Then blessed be God, the Lord of the Worlds! (Al-Ghafir, 40:64)

Nay, but those who do wrong follow their own lusts without knowledge. Who is able to guide him whom God hath sent astray? For such there are no helpers. So set thy purpose (O Muhammad) for religion as a man by nature upright – the nature (framed) of God, in which He hath created man. There is no altering (the laws of) God's creation. That is the right religion, but most men know not— (Al-Rum, 30:29-30)

And when I have fashioned him and breathed into him of My Spirit, then fall down before him prostrate, (Sad, 38:72)

And when thy Lord said unto the angels: Lo! I am about to place a viceroy in the earth, they said: Wilt thou place therein one who will do harm therein and will shed blood, while we, we hymn Thy praise and sanctify Thee? He said: Surely I know that which ye know not. And He taught Adam all the names, then showed them to the angels, saying: Inform Me of the names of these, if ye are truthful. They said: Be glorified! We have no knowledge saving that which Thou hast taught us. Lo! Thou, only Thou, art the Knower, the Wise. He said: O Adam! Inform them of their names, and when he had informed them of their names, He said: Did I not tell you that I know the secret of the heavens and the earth? And I know that which ye disclose and which ye hide. And when We said unto the angels: Prostrate yourselves before Adam, they fell prostrate, all save Iblis. He demurred through pride, and so became a disbeliever... And We said: O Adam! Dwell thou and thy wife in the Garden, and eat ye freely (of the fruits) thereof where ye will; but come not nigh this tree lest ye become wrong-doers. (Al-Baqarah, 2:30-35)

xviii *Sahih Al-Bukhari, Kitab al-Iman, Hadith* no.13.

xix *Sahih Muslim, Kitab al-Iman, 67-1, Hadith* no.45.

xx The classical commentators on the Holy Qur'an (see: *Tafsir Ibn Kathir, Tafsir Al-Jalalayn*) generally agree that this is a reference to (the last movements of) the Muslim prayer.

xxi Abu Ja'far Muhammad ibn Jarir Al-Tabari, *Jami' al-Bayan fi Ta'wil al-Qur'an, (Dar al-Kutub al-'Ilmiyyah*, Beirut, Lebanon, 1st ed, 1992/1412,) *tafsir* of *Aal-'Imran,* 3:64;Volume 3, pp. 299-302.

xxii According to grammarians cited by Tabari (op cit.) the word 'common' (*sawa'*) in 'a common word between us' also means 'just', 'fair' (*adl*).

xxiii The Blessed Theophylact (1055-1108 C.E.) was the Orthodox Archbishop of Ochrid and Bulgaria (1090-1108 C.E.). His native language was the Greek of the New Testament. His *Commentary* is currently available in English from Chrysostom Press.

SIGNATORIES
(in Alphabetical Order)

1 His Royal Eminence Sultan Muhammadu Sa'ad Ababakar
   The 20th Sultan of Sokoto; Leader of the Muslims of Nigeria
2 H.E. Shaykh Dr. Hussein Hasan Abakar
   Imam of the Muslims, Chad; President, Higher Council for Islamic Affairs, Chad
3 H.E. Prof. Dr. Abdul-Salam Al-Abbadi
   President of Aal Al-Bayt University; Former Minister of Religious Affairs, Jordan
4 Prof. Dr. Taha Abd Al-Rahman
   President of the Wisdom Circle for Thinkers and Researchers, Morocco; Director of Al-Umma Al-Wasat Magazine, International Union of Muslim Scholars
5 Imam Feisal Abdul Rauf
   Co-founder and Chairman of the Board of the Cordoba Initiative; Founder of the ASMA Society (American Society for Muslim Advancement); Imam of Masjid Al-Farah, NY, NY, USA
6 Sheikh Muhammad Nur Abdullah
   Vice President of the Fiqh Council of North America, USA
7 Dr. Shaykh Abd Al-Quddus Abu Salah
   President of the International League for Islamic Ethics; Editor of the Journal for Islamic Ethics, Riyadh, Saudi Arabia
8 H.E. Prof. Dr. Abd Al-Wahhab bin Ibrahim Abu Solaiman
   Member of the Committee of Senior Ulama, Saudi Arabia
9 Dr. Lateef Oladimeji Adegbite
   Acting Secretary and Legal Adviser, Nigerian Supreme Council for Islamic Affairs
10 H.E. Amb. Prof. Dr. Akbar Ahmed
   Ibn Khaldun Chair of Islamic Studies, American University in Washington D.C., USA

11 H.E. Judge Prince Bola Ajibola
    Former International High Court Judge; Former Minister of Justice
    of Nigeria; Former Attorney-General of Nigeria; Founder of the Crescent
    University and Founder of the Islamic Movement of Africa (IMA)

12 H.E. Prof. Dr. Kamil Al-Ajlouni
    Head of National Centre for Diabetes; Founder of the Jordanian University
    of Science and Technology (JUST), Former Minister and Former Senator,
    Jordan

13 Shaykh Dr. Mohammed Salim Al-'Awa
    Secretary General of the International Union of Muslim Scholars; Head of
    the Egyptian Association for Culture and Dialogue

14 Mr. Nihad Awad
    National Executive Director and Co-founder of the Council on American-
    Islamic Relations (CAIR), USA

15 H.E. Prof. Dr. Al-Hadi Al-Bakkoush
    Former Prime Minister of Tunisia, Author

16 H.E. Shaykh Al-Islam Dr. Allah-Shakur bin Hemmat Bashazada
    Grand Mufti of Azerbaijan and Head of the Muslim Administration of the
    Caucasus

17 H.E. Dr. Issam El-Bashir
    Secretary General of the International Moderation Centre, Kuwait; Former
    Minister of Religious Affairs, Sudan

18 H.E. Prof. Dr. *Allamah* Shaykh Abd Allah bin Mahfuz bin Bayyah
    Professor, King Abdul Aziz University, Saudi Arabia; Former Minister of
    Justice, Former Minister of Education and Former Minister of Religious
    Affairs, Mauritania; Vice President of the International Union of Muslim
    Scholars; Founder and President, Global Center for Renewal and Guidance

19 Dr. Mohamed Bechari
    President, Federal Society for Muslims in France; General Secretary of the
    European Islamic Conference (EIC), France; Member of the International
    Fiqh Academy

20 Prof. Dr. Ahmed Chaouki Binbine
    Director of the Hasaniyya Library, Morocco

21 Prof. Dr. *Allamah* Shaykh Muhammad Sa'id Ramadan Al-Buti
    Dean, Dept. of Religion, University of Damascus, Syria

22 Prof. Dr. Mustafa Çağrıcı
    Mufti of Istanbul, Turkey

23 H.E. Shaykh Prof. Dr. Mustafa Cerić
    Grand Mufti and Head of Ulema of Bosnia and Herzegovina

24 Professor Ibrahim Chabbuh
    Director General of the Royal Aal al-Bayt Institute for Islamic Thought,

Jordan; President of the Association for the Safeguarding of the City of Qayrawan, Tunisia

25 H.E. Prof. Dr. Mustafa Cherif
Muslim Intellectual; Former Minister of Higher Education and Former Ambassador, Algeria

26 Dr. Caner Dagli
Assistant Professor, Roanoke College, USA

27 Ayatollah Prof. Dr. *Seyyed* Mostafa Mohaghegh Damad
Dean of Department of Islamic Studies, The Academy of Sciences of Iran; Professor of Law and Islamic Philosophy, Tehran University; Fellow, The Iranian Academy of Sciences, Iran; Former Inspector General of Iran

28 Ayatollah *Seyyed* Abu Al-Qasim Al-Deebaji
Imam Zayn Al-Abideen Mosque, Kuwait

29 H.E. Prof. Dr. Shakir Al-Fahham
Head of the Arabic Language Academy, Damascus; Former Minister of Education, Syria

30 Shaykh *Seyyed* Hani Fahs
Member of Supreme Shia Committee, Lebanon; Founding Member of the Arab Committee for the Islamic-Christian Dialogue, and the Permanent Committee for the Lebanese Dialogue

31 H.E. Shaykh Salim Falahat
Director General of the Muslim Brotherhood, Jordan

32 *Chief* Abdul Wahab Iyanda Folawiyo
Member, Supreme Council for Islamic Affairs of Nigeria; Vice President, Jamaat Nasril Islam

33 H.E. Shaykh Ravil Gainutdin
Grand Mufti of Russia

34 Justice Ibrahim Kolapo Sulu Gambari
Justice of Nigerian Court of Appeal; National Vice Chairman, Nigerian Football Association (NFA)

35 Prof. Dr. Abd Al-Karim Gharaybeh
Historian and Senator, Jordan

36 H.E. Prof. Dr. Abdullah Yusuf Al-Ghoneim
Director of the Kuwaiti Centre for Research and Studies on Kuwait; Former Minister of Education, Kuwait

37 H.E. Prof. Dr. Bouabdellah Ghlamallah
Minister of Religious Affairs, Algeria

38 Prof. Dr. Alan Godlas
Co-Chair, Islamic Studies, University of Georgia, USA; Editor-in-chief, Sufi News and Sufism World Report; Director, Sufis Without Borders

39 H.E. Shaykh Nedžad Grabus

Grand Mufti of Slovenia

40 H.E. Shaykh Dr. *Al-Habib* Ahmad bin Abd Al-Aziz Al-Haddad
Chief Mufti of Dubai, UAE

41 Shaykh *Al-Habib* Ali Mashhour bin Muhammad bin Salim bin
Hafeeth
Imam of the Tarim Mosque and Head of Fatwa Council, Tarim, Yemen

42 Shaykh *Al-Habib* Umar bin Muhammad bin Salim bin Hafeeth
Dean, Dar Al-Mustafa, Tarim, Yemen

43 Professor Dr. Farouq Hamadah
Professor of the Sciences of Tradition, Mohammad V University, Morocco

44 Shaykh Hamza Yusuf Hanson
Founder and Director, Zaytuna Institute, CA, USA

45 H.E. Shaykh Dr. Ahmad Badr Al-Din Hassoun
Grand Mufti of the Republic of Syria

46 H.E. Shaykh *Sayyed* Ali bin Abd Al-Rahman Al-Hashimi
Advisor to the President for Judiciary and Religious Affairs, UAE

47 Prof. Dr. Hasan Hanafi
Muslim Intellectual, Department of Philosophy, Cairo University

48 Shaykh Kabir Helminski
Shaykh of the Mevlevi Tariqah; Co-Director of the Book Foundation, USA

49 H.E. Shaykh Sa'id Hijjawi
Chief Scholar, The Royal Aal al-Bayt Institute for Islamic Thought; Former Grand Mufti of Jordan

50 H.E. Prof. Dr. Shaykh Ahmad Hlayyel
Chief Islamic Justice of Jordan; Imam of the Hashemite Court; Former Minister of Religious Affairs

51 H.E. Amb. Dr. Murad Hofmann
Author and Muslim Intellectual, Germany

52 H.E. Dr. Anwar Ibrahim
Former Deputy Prime Minister of Malaysia; Honorary President of AccountAbility

53 H.E. Shaykh Dr. Ezzedine Ibrahim
Advisor for Cultural Affairs, Prime Ministry, UAE

54 H.E. Prof. Dr. Ekmeleddin Ihsanoğlu
Secretary-General, Organization of the Islamic Conference (OIC)

55 H.E. Prof. Dr. Omar Jah
Secretary of the Muslim Scholars Council, Gambia; Professor of Islamic Civilization and Thought, University of Gambia

56 H.E. Prof. Dr. Abbas Jrari
Advisor to HM the King, Morocco

57 Shaykh *Al-Habib* Ali Zain Al-Abidin Al-Jifri
Founder and Director, Taba Institute, United Arab Emirates

58 H.E. Shaykh Prof. Dr. Ali Jumʻa
Grand Mufti of the Republic of Egypt

59 Prof. Dr. Yahya Mahmud bin Junayd
Secretary General, King Faisal Centre for Research and Islamic Studies,
Saudi Arabia

60 Dr. Ibrahim Kalin
Director, SETA Foundation, Ankara, Turkey; Asst. Prof. Georgetown
University, USA

61 H.E. Amb. Aref Kamal
Muslim Intellectual, Pakistan

62 Professor Dr. ʻAbla Mohammed Kahlawi
Dean of Islamic and Arabic Studies, Al-Azhar University (Women's
College), Egypt

63 Prof. Dr. Said Hibatullah Kamilev
Director, Moscow Institute of Islamic Civilisation, Russian Federation

64 Prof. Dr. *Hafiz* Yusuf Z. Kavakci
Resident Scholar, Islamic Association of North Texas, Founder & Instructor
of IANT Qur'anic Academy; Founding Dean of Suffa Islamic Seminary,
Dallas, Texas, USA

65 Shaykh Dr. Nuh Ha Mim Keller
Shaykh in the Shadhili Order, USA

66 Prof. Dr. Mohammad Hashim Kamali
Dean and Professor, International Institute of Islamic Thought and
Civilization (ISTAC), International Islamic University, Malaysia

67 Shaykh Amr Khaled
Islamic Missionary, Preacher and Broadcaster, Egypt; Founder and
Chairman, Right Start Foundation International

68 Prof. Dr. Abd Al-Karim Khalifah
President of the Jordanian Arabic Language Academy; Former President of
Jordan University

69 H.E. Shaykh Ahmad Al-Khalili
Grand Mufti of the Sultanate of Oman

70 *Seyyed* Jawad Al-Khoei
Secretary-General, Al-Khoei International Foundation

71 Shaykh Dr. Ahmad Kubaisi
Founder of the ʻUlema Organization, Iraq

72 Mr. M. Ali Lakhani
Founder and Editor of Sacred Web: A Journal of Tradition and Modernity,
Canada

73 Dr. Joseph Lumbard
    Assistant Professor, Brandeis University, USA
74 H.E. Shaykh Mahmood A. Madani
    Secretary General, Jamiat Ulama-i-Hind; Member of Parliament, India
75 H.E. Prof. Dr. Abdelkebir Alaoui M'Daghri
    Director General of Bayt Mal Al-Quds Agency (Al-Quds Fund); Former
    Minister of Religious Affairs, Morocco
76 H.E. *Imam Sayyed* Al-Sadiq Al-Mahdi
    Former Prime Minister of Sudan; Head of Ansar Movement, Sudan
77 H.E. Prof. Dr. Rusmir Mahmutcehajić
    Professor, Sarajevo University; President of the International Forum Bosnia;
    Former Vice President of the Government of Bosnia and Herzegovina
78 *Allamah* Shaykh *Sayyed* Muhammad bin Muhammad Al-Mansour
    High Authority (Marja') of Zeidi Muslims, Yemen
79 Prof. Dr. Bashshar Awwad Marouf
    Former Rector of the Islamic University, Iraq
80 H.E. Prof. Dr. Ahmad Matloub
    Former Minister of Culture; Acting President of the Iraqi Academy of
    Sciences, Iraq
81 Prof. Dr. Ingrid Mattson
    Professor of Islamic Studies and Christian-Muslim Relations and Director,
    Islamic Chaplaincy Program, Hartford Seminary; President of the Islamic
    Society of North America (ISNA), USA
82 Dr. Yousef Meri
    Special Scholar-in-Residence, Royal Aal al-Bayt Institute for Islamic
    Thought, Jordan
83 Dr. Jean-Louis Michon
    Author; Muslim Scholar; Architect; Former UNESCO expert,
    Switzerland
84 Shaykh Abu Bakr Ahmad Al-Milibari
    Secretary-General of the Ahl Al-Sunna Association, India
85 Pehin Dato Haj Suhaili bin Haj Mohiddin
    Deputy Grand Mufti, Brunei
86 Ayatollah Sheikh Hussein Muayad
    President and Founder, Knowledge Forum, Baghdad, Iraq
87 Prof. Dr. Izzedine Umar Musa
    Professor of Islamic History, King Sa'ud University, Saudi Arabia
88 Prof. Dr. Mohammad Farouk Al-Nabhan
    Former Director of Dar Al-Hadith Al-Hasaniya, Morocco
89 Prof. Dr. Zaghloul El-Naggar
    Professor, King Abd Al-Aziz University, Jeddah, Saudi Arabia; Head,

Committee on Scientific Facts in the Glorious Qur'an, Supreme Council on Islamic Affairs, Egypt

90 Mr. Sohail Nakhooda
Editor-in-Chief, Islamica Magazine, Jordan

91 Prof. Dr. Hisham Nashabeh
Chairman of the Board of Higher Education; Dean of Education at Makassed Association, Lebanon

92 H.E. Professor Dr. *Seyyed* Hossein Nasr
University Professor of Islamic Studies, George Washington University, Washington D.C, USA

93 Prof. Dr. Aref Ali Nayed
Former Professor at the Pontifical Institute for Arabic and Islamic Studies (Rome); Former Professor at International Institute for Islamic Thought and Civilization (ISTAC, Malaysia); Senior Advisor to the Cambridge Interfaith Program at the Faculty of Divinity in Cambridge, UK

94 H.E. Shaykh Ševki Omarbašić
Grand Mufti of Croatia

95 Dato Dr. Abdul Hamid Othman
Advisor to the H.E. the Prime Minister of Malaysia

96 Prof. Dr. Ali Özek
Head of the Endowment for Islamic Scientific Studies, Istanbul, Turkey

97 Imam Yahya Sergio Yahe Pallavicini
Vice President of CO.RE.IS., Italy, Chairman of ISESCO Council for Education and Culture in the West, Advisor for Islamic Affairs of the Italian Minister of Interior.

98 H.E. Shaykh Dr. Nuh Ali Salman Al-Qudah
Grand Mufti of the Hashemite Kingdom of Jordan

99 H.E. Shaykh Dr. Ikrima Said Sabri
Former Grand Mufti of Jerusalem and All of Palestine, Imam of the Blessed Al-Aqsa Mosque, and President of the Islamic Higher Council, Palestine

100 Ayatollah Al-Faqih *Seyyed* Hussein Ismail Al-Sadr
Baghdad, Iraq

101 Mr. Muhammad Al-Sammak
Secretary-General of the National Council for Islamic-Christian Dialogue; Secretary-General for the Islamic Spiritual Summit, Lebanon

102 Shaykh *Seyyed* Hasan Al-Saqqaf
Director of Dar Al-Imam Al-Nawawi, Jordan

103 Dr. Ayman Fuad Sayyid
Historian and Manuscript Expert, Former Secretary General of Dar al-Kutub Al-Misriyya, Cairo, Egypt

104 Prof. Dr. Suleiman Abdallah Schleifer

Professor Emeritus, The American University in Cairo

105 Dr. *Seyyed* Reza Shah-Kazemi
Author and Muslim Scholar, UK

106 Dr. Anas Al-Shaikh-Ali
Chair, Association of Muslim Social Scientists, UK; Chair, Forum Against Islamophobia and Racism, UK; Academic Advisor, IIIT, UK

107 Imam Zaid Shakir
Lecturer and Scholar-in-Residence, Zaytuna Institute, CA, USA

108 H.E. Prof. Dr. Ali Abdullah Al-Shamlan
Director General of the Kuwait Foundation for the Advancement of Sciences (KFAS); Former Minister of Higher Education, Kuwait

109 Eng. *Seyyed* Hasan Shariatmadari
Leader of the Iranian National Republican Party (INR)

110 Dr. Muhammad Alwani Al-Sharif
Head of the European Academy of Islamic Culture and Sciences, Brussels, Belgium

111 H.E. Dr. Mohammad Abd Al-Ghaffar Al-Sharif
Secretary-General of the Ministry of Religious Affairs, Kuwait

112 Dr. Tayba Hassan Al-Sharif
International Protection Officer, The United Nations High Commissioner for Refugees, Darfur, Sudan

113 Prof. Dr. Muhammad bin Sharifa
Former Rector of Wajda University; Morocco; Fellow of the Royal Moroccan Academy

114 Prof. Dr. Muzammil H. Siddiqui on behalf of the whole Fiqh Council of North America
Islamic Scholar and Theologian; Chairman of the Fiqh Council of North America, USA

115 Shaykh Ahmad bin Sa'ud Al-Siyabi
Secretary General of the Directorate of the Grand Mufti, Oman

116 Al-Haji Yusuf Maitama Sule
Former Nigerian Permanent Representative to the United Nations; Former Nigerian Minister of National Guidance

117 Prof. Dr. Muhammad Abd Al-Rahim Sultan-al-Ulama
Deputy-Dean of Scientific Research Affairs, United Arab Emirates University, UAE

118 Shaykh Dr. Tariq Sweidan
Director-General of the Risalah Satellite Channel

119 H.E. Shaykh Ahmad Muhammad Muti'i Tamim
The Head of the Religious Administration of Ukrainian Muslims, and Mufti of Ukraine

120 H.E. Shaykh Izz Al-Din Al-Tamimi
Senator; Former Chief Islamic Justice, Minister of Religious Affairs and Grand Mufti of Jordan

121 H.E. Shaykh Dr. Tayseer Rajab Al-Tamimi
Chief Islamic Justice of Palestine; Head of The Palestinian Center for Religion and Civilization Dialogue

122 Prof. Dr. H.R.H. Prince Ghazi bin Muhammad bin Talal
Personal Envoy and Special Advisor of H.M. King Abdullah II; Chairman of the Board of the Royal Aal al-Bayt Institute for Islamic Thought, Jordan

123 Prof. Dr. Ammar Al-Talibi
Former Member of Parliament, Professor of Philosophy, University of Algeria

124 Ayatollah Shaykh Muhammad Ali Taskhiri
Secretary General of the World Assembly for Proximity of Islamic Schools of Thought (WAPIST), Iran

125 H.E. Prof. Dr. Shaykh Ahmad Muhammad Al-Tayeb
President of Al-Azhar University, Former Grand Mufti of Egypt

126 Prof. Dr. Muddathir Abdel-Rahim Al-Tayib
Professor of Political Science and Islamic Studies, International Institute of Islamic Thought and Civilization (ISTAC), Malaysia

127 H.E. Amb. Prof. Dr. Abdel-Hadi Al-Tazi
Fellow of the Royal Moroccan Academy

128 H.E. Shaykh Naim Trnava
Grand Mufti of Kosovo

129 H.E. Dr. Abd Al-Aziz bin 'Uthman Al-Tweijiri
Director-General of the Islamic Educational, Scientific and Cultural Organization (ISESCO)

130 H.E. Prof. Dr. Nasaruddin Umar
Rector of the Institute for Advanced Qur'anic Studies; Secretary General of the Nahdhatul Ulama Consultative Council; Lecturer at the State Islamic University Syarif Hidayatullah, Jakarta, Indonesia

131 Shaykh Muhammad Hasan 'Usayran
Jafari Mufti of Sidon and Al-Zahrani, Lebanon

132 *Allamah* Justice Mufti Muhammad Taqi Usmani
Vice President, Darul Uloom Karachi, Pakistan

133 Prof. Dr. Akhtarul Wasey
Director, Zakir Husain Institute of Islamic Studies, Jamia Milla Islamiya University, India

134 Shaykh Abdal Hakim Murad Winter
Shaykh Zayed Lecturer in Islamic Studies, Divinity School, University of Cambridge; Director of the Muslim Academic Trust, UK

135 Prof. Dr. Mohammed El-Mokhtar Ould Bah
President, Chinguitt Modern University, Mauritania

136 H.E. Shaykh Muhammad Sodiq Mohammad Yusuf
Former Grand Mufti of the Muslim Spiritual Administration of Central Asia, Uzbekistan; Translator and Commentator of the Holy Qur'an

137 Prof. Dr. Shaykh Wahba Mustafa Al-Zuhayli
Dean, Department of Islamic Jurisprudence, University of Damascus, Syria

138 H.E. Shaykh Muamer Zukorlić
Mufti of Sandžak

139 Shaikh Ahmad Kutty (Toronto) *October 13, 2007*

140 Dr. M. Saud Anwar (Co-Chair, American Muslim Peace Initiative) *October 13, 2007*

141 Amir Hussain, PhD (Associate Professor of Theological Studies, Loyola Marymount University, Los Angeles) *October 14, 2007*

142 Dr. Hisham A. Hellyer (Senior Research Fellow, University of Warwick, UK) *October 15, 2007*

143 Mehrézia Labidi-Maiza (International Co-ordinator of Religious Women for Peace Network) *October 18, 2007*

144 Professor Tariq Ramadan (European Muslim Network (EMN), Brussels) *October 26, 2007*

145 Shaykh Faraz Rabbani (Hanafi Scholar, Sunnipath.com) *November 6, 2007*

146 Imam Abdul Malik Mujahid (Chairman of the Council of Islamic Organizations of Greater Chicago) *November 17, 2007*

147 Prof. Dr. Najib al-Hsadi (Professor of Philosophy, Gar Yunis University, Benghazi Libya) *December 25, 2007*

148 Prof. Dr. Basit Koshul (Lahore University of Management Sciences, Pakistan) *December 25, 2007*

149 Dr. Muhammad Suheyl Umar (Director, Iqbal Academy, Pakistan) *December 25, 2007*

150 Prof. Dr. Muhammad Fathullah Al-Ziadi (Dean, Islamic Call College, Tripoli, Libya) *December 25, 2007*

151 Prof. Dr. Muhammad Ahmed al-Sharif (Director, World Islamic Call Society, Tripoli, Libya) *December 25, 2007*

152 Dr. Zumer Saleh (Religious Leader of Albanian Community in London) *December 25, 2007*

153 Shaykha Yasmin Mahmud Al-Husary (Head of Husary Islamic Foundation, Egypt) *December 25, 2007*

154 Shaykh Dr. Usama Al-Rifaei (Mufti of Akkar, Lebanon) *December 25, 2007*

155 Sayyed Umar Ibn Hamed Al-Jailani (Chief Jurist and Scholar, Yemen) *December 25, 2007*

156 Dr. Umar Abdul-Kafi (Prominent Caller to Islamic Faith, Egypt) *December 25, 2007*

157 Shaykh Seid Smajkić (Mufti of Mostar, Bosnia-Herzegovina) *December 25, 2007*

158 H.H. Shaikh Salem Ibn Mohammad Al-Qasimi (Chairman of Islamic Forum, Sharjah, U.A.E.) *December 25, 2007*

159 Dr. Saleha Rhouti (Professor & Researcher, Faculty of Arts, Rabat, Morocco) *December 25, 2007*

160 Dr. Salah Al-Din Kuftaro (Chairman of 'Shaykh Ahmad Kuftaro' Foundation, Damascus, Syria) *December 25, 2007*

161 Shaykh Salah Al-Din Fakhri (Director of 'Azhar of Lebanon', Lebanon) *December 25, 2007*

162 Shaykh Saad Allah Al-Barzanji (Prominent Scholar, Iraq) *December 25, 2007*

163 Shaykh Rifat Fejzić (Chairman of the Islamic Organization of Montenegro) *December 25, 2007*

164 Dr. Ramiz Zekaj (Director-General, Albanian Institute for Islamic Thought & Civilisation, Tirane, Albania) *December 25, 2007*

165 Dr. Qais ibn Mohammad Aal Mubarak (Associate Professor of Jurisprudence, Faculty of Education, Al-Ahsa, Saudi Arabia) *December 25, 2007*

166 Shaykh Nusrat Abdibegović (Mufti of Travnik, Bosnia) *December 25, 2007*

167 Prof. Dr. Nasr Aref (Head of Islamic Studies Department, Zayed University, Abu Dhabi) *December 25, 2007*

168 Prof. Dr. Najib al-Hsadi (Professor of Philosophy, Gar Yunis University, Benghazi, Libya) *December 25, 2007*

169 Shaykh Nafiullah Ashirov (Mufti of the Asian Provinces of Russia) *December 25, 2007*

170 Dr. Moulay Al-Hussein Alhyan (Professor, Al-Qarawiyyin University, Fez, Morocco) *December 25, 2007*

171 Shaykh Muhammed Abdullah B. Qarachay (Deputy Mufti of Russian Federation) *December 25, 2007*

172 Dr. Mohammad Rashid Qabbani (Grand Mufti of Lebanon) *December 25, 2007*

173 Dr. Mohammad Rabi'e Al-Nadwi (Chairman of Nadwat Al Ulama, India) *December 25, 2007*

174 Dr. Mohammad Mattar Al-Qa'bi (Director, Abu Dhabi

Religious Affairs Authority, U.A.E.) *December 25, 2007*

175 Dr. Mohammad Kharobat (Professor, Cadi Ayyad University, Marrakesh, Morocco) *December 25, 2007*

176 Dr. Mohammad Hasan Shurahbili (Professor, Al-Qurawiyyin University, Fez, Morocco) *December 25, 2007*

177 Dr. Mohammad Benkirane (Professor, Ibn Tofayl University Kénitra, Morocco) *December 25, 2007*

178 Dr. Moulouda Cham (Professor, the Law College in Rabat, Morocco) *December 25, 2007*

179 Dr. Maimoune Bariche (Professor, Cadi Ayyad University, Marrakesh, Morocco) *December 25, 2007*

180 Dr. Larbi Kachat (Director of Dawah Mosque and Head of the Islamic Cultural Center, Paris) *December 25, 2007*

181 Shaykh Khaled Al-Sulh (Mufti of Baalbek, Lebanon) *December 25, 2007*

182 Shaykh Jihad Hashim Brown (Director of Research, Tabah Foundation, U.S.A.) *December 25, 2007*

183 Prof. Dr. Jassem Ali Al-Shamsi (Dean, Shariah College, U.A.E. University, U.A.E.) *December 25, 2007*

184 Dr. Jamal Farouk (Professor of Religions and Sects, Faculty of Islamic Da'wa, Al-Azhar University Egypt) *December 25, 2007*

185 Shaykh Ismail Smajlović (Mufti of the Armed Forces of Bosnia-Herzegovina) *December 25, 2007*

186 Dr. Ibrahim Bumilha (Head of Organizing Committee of Holy Quran Dubai International Award U.A.E.) *December 25, 2007*

187 Shaykh Husein Smajić (Mufti of Sarajevo) *December 25, 2007*

188 Shaykh Hussein Kavazović (Mufti of Tuzla, Bosnia-Herzegovina) *December 25, 2007*

189 Shaykh Hasan Makić (Mufti of Bihać, Bosnia-Herzegovina) *December 25, 2007*

190 Prof. Dr. Hani Sulayman Al-Tu'aymat (Dean, Shariah and Islamic Studies, U.A.E. University, Jordan) *December 25, 2007*

191 Prof. Dr. Hamed Ahmad Al-Refaie (President of World Islamic Forum for Dialogue, Saudi Arabia) *December 25, 2007*

192 Shaykh Hamed Efendić (Mufti of Goražde, Bosnia-Herzegovina) *December 25, 2007*

193 Dr. Hamdan M. Al-Mazroui (Chairman of Abu Dhabi Religious Affairs Authority, U.A.E.) *December 25, 2007*

194 Dr. Buthayna Al-Galbzuri (Professor & Researcher, Faculty of Arts, Rabat, Morocco) *December 25, 2007*

195 Dr. Bassem H. Itani (Director, Dar Iqra for Islamic Sciences;

Member of the Administrative Board of the Guidance and Reform Trust, Beirut, Lebanon) *December 25, 2007*

196 Shaykh Ismat Spahic (Deputy Head of 'Ulama of Bosnia and Herzegovina) *December 25, 2007*

197 Dr. Asmat Mojaddedi (Chairman of the Muslim Council of Denmark (MFR)), *December 25, 2007*

198 Dr. Jilali El Mrini (Professor, Sidi Mohammed Benabdellah University, Fez, Morocco) *December 25, 2007*

199 Dr. Ali Benbraik (Professor, Ibn Zohr University, Agadir, Morocco) *December 25, 2007*

200 Dr. Al-Betoul Binali (Professor & Researcher, Faculty of Arts, Rabat, Morocco) *December 25, 2007*

201 Dr. Larbi Buselham (Professor, Mohammad V University, Rabat, Morocco) *December 25, 2007*

202 Dr. Larbi Al-Buhali (Professor, Cadi Ayyad University, Marrakesh, Morocco) *December 25, 2007*

203 Shaykh Ejup Davutović (Mufti of Zenica, Bosnia-Herzegovina) *December 25, 2007*

204 Dr. Aisha Y. Al-Manna'ie (Dean, Faculty of Shariah and Islamic Studies, University of Qatar, Doha, Qatar) *December 25, 2007*

205 Dr. Ahmad Omar Hashim (Former President, Azhar University; Head of Religious Committee, Egyptian People's Council) *December 25, 2007*

206 Dr. Ahmad Mihrizi (Professor, Cadi Ayyad University, Marrakech, Morocco) December 25, 2007

207 Dr. Ahmad Fakir (Professor, Ibn Zohr University, Agadir, Morocco) *December 25, 2007*

208 Shaykh Edhem Šamdĉić (Mufti of Banja Luka, Bosnia-Herzegovina) *December 25, 2007*

209 Dr. Abdul-Razzaq Hirmas (Professor, Ibn Zohr University, Agadir, Morocco) *December 25, 2007*

210 Dr. Abdul-Rafi'e Al-Ilj (Professor, Moulay Ismail University, Meknes Morocco) *December 25, 2007*

211 Dr. Abdul-Nasser Jabri (Dean, Islamic Call College, Beirut) *December 25, 2007*

212 Dr. Abdul-Mu'ti Bayyoumi (Member of the Academy of Islamic Research, Al-Azhar University, Cairo) *December 25, 2007*

213 Sayyed Abdullah ibn Mohammad Fad'aq (Caller to the Faith, Mecca) *December 25, 2007*

214 Dr. Abdul-Hakim Ikaiwi (Professor, Ibn Zohr University,

Aghadir, Morocco) *December 25, 2007*

215   Dr. Abdul-Fattah Al-Bizm (Mufti of Damascus; Director of Al-Fath Islamic Institute, Syria) *December 25, 2007*

216   Dr. Abdul-Aziz Al-Hafadhi (Research Professor, Mohammed V University, Oujda, Morocco) *December 25, 2007*

217   Dr. Agel Elmeri (World Islamic Call Society, Tripoli) *January 06, 2008*

218   Prof. Dr. Marcia Hermansen (Professor of Islamic Studies, Loyola University, USA) *January 06, 2008*

219   Prof. Fadel Abdullah (Lecturer in Arabic and Translation Studies) *January 06, 2008*

220   Dr. Ghada Talhami (Professor of Politics, Lake Furest College, Illinois USA.) *January 06, 2008*

221   Dr. Assad Bussoul (Professor and Chairman: Arabic Department. American Islamic College, Chicago, USA) *January 06, 2008*

222   Prof. Dr. Mahmoud Abul-Futouh al-Sayyid (Former Chairman, Department of Religions and Sects, Faculty of Islamic Da'wa, Al-Azhar University, Cairo) *January 13, 2008*

223   Prof. Dr. Mohammad Mahmoud Mitwalli Abdul-Barr (Professor, Department of Islamic Culture, Faculty of Islamic Da'wa, Al-Azhar University, Cairo) *January 13, 2008*

224   Prof. Dr. Mohammad Abdul-Hadi Imam (Professor, Department of Religions and Sects, Faculty of Islamic Da'wa, Al-Azhar University, Cairo) *January 13, 2008*

225   Prof. Dr. Abdul-Basit al-Sayyid al-Mursi (Professor, Department of Islamic Culture, Faculty of Islamic Da'wa, Al-Azhar University, Cairo) *January 13, 2008*

226   Prof. Dr. Mohammad Ibrahim al-Geyoushi (Ex-Dean, Faculty of Islamic Da'wa, Al-Azhar University, Cairo) *January 13, 2008*

227   Prof. Dr. Tal'at Mohammad Afifi (Ex-Dean, Faculty of Islamic Da'wa, Al-Azhar University, Cairo) *January 13, 2008*

228   Prof. Dr. Adil Mohammad Mohammad Darwish (Professor, Department of Religions and Sects, Faculty of Islamic Da'wa, Al-Azhar University, Cairo) *January 13, 2008*

229   Prof. Dr. Adil Mahmoud Abdul-Khaliq (Professor, Department of Islamic Culture, Faculty of Islamic Da'wa, Al-Azhar University, Cairo) *January 13, 2008*

230   Prof. Dr. Hasan Jabr Hasan Shuqair (Dean, Faculty of Islamic Da'wa, Al-Azhar University, Cairo) *January 13, 2008*

231   Prof. Dr. Abdullah Abdul-Hameed Samak (Chairman,

Department of Religions and Sects, Faculty of Islamic Da'wa, Al-Azhar University, Cairo) *January 13, 2008*

232 Prof. Dr. Ahmed Mohammad Ibrahim Shihatah (Professor, Department of Islamic Culture, Faculty of Islamic Da'wa, Al-Azhar University, Cairo) *January 13, 2008*

233 Prof. Dr. Ahmed Rabi' Ahmed Yousef (Dean, Faculty of Islamic Da'wa, Al-Azhar University, Cairo) *January 13, 2008*

234 Prof. Dr. Din Syamsuddin (President, Central Board of Muhammadiyah, Indonesia) *February 16, 2008*

235 Maher Hathout (Senior Advisor, Muslim Public Affairs Council, Los Angeles, USA) *February 20, 2008*

236 Salam Al-Marayati (Executive Director, Muslim Public Affairs Council, Los Angeles, USA) *February 20, 2008*

237 Amina Rasul (Lead Convenor, Philippine Council for Islam and Democracy, Mandaluyong City, Philippines) *February 20, 2008*

238 Latifa Al. Al-Busseir (Executive Manager, HRH Prince Alwaleed bin Talal Bin Abdulaziz Alsaud Kingdom Foundation, Saudi Arabia) *February 23, 2008*

239 Muna AbuSulayman (Executive Director, HRH Prince Alwaleed bin Talal Bin Abdulaziz Alsaud Kingdom Foundation, Saudi Arabia) *February 23, 2008*

240 Prof Dr. Shahrzad Houshmand Zadeh (Professor of Islamic Studies and Muslim-Christian Relations, The Institute for Studies on Religions and Cultures, The Pontifical Gregorian University, Rome) *March 05, 2008*

241 Prof. Dr. Adnane Mokrani (Professor of Islamic Studies and Muslim-Christian Relations, The Institute for Studies on Religions and Cultures, The Pontifical Gregorian University, Rome) *March 05, 2008*

242 Congressman Keith Ellison (The Fifth Congressional District of Minnesota, United States House of Representatives) *March 09, 2008*

243 Prof. Dr. Hmida Ennaifer (Professor of Islamic Theology, al-Zaytuna University, Tunis. Muslim Co-President of the Muslim-Christian Research Group (GRIC). Founder of *15/21, Magazine of Intercultural Dialogue* (Tunis).) *March 13, 2008*

244 Anouar N. Haddam (Member-Elect of the Algerian Parliament (FIS list, Dec. 1991); President, Movement for Liberty and Social Justice, Algeria) *March 15, 2008*

245 Dr Naveed. S. Shaykh, Lecturer in International Relations, Keele University, UK *April 14, 2008*

246 Prof. M.A.S. Abdel Haleem, Director Centre of Islamic
 Studies School of Oriental and African Studies). *May 10, 2008*

247 Dr Fareeha Khan (Assistant Professor of Islam, Department
 of Religion, Georgia State University)

248 Ayesha Siddiqua Chaudhry (Department of Middle Eastern
 and Islamic Studies, New York University)

249 HRH Princess Dr Areej Ghazi (Founder and Director, The
 School of Life, Jordan) *June 2, 2008*

250 Mr Mohammed Ali (CEO, Islam Channel, London, UK) *June
 8, 2008*

251 Dr. Musharraf Hussain Al-Azhari (Director, Karimia
 Institute, Nottingham, UK) *June 8, 2008*

252 Mr Salah Algafrawi (Assistant Secretary-General for the
 Islamic European Conference, Germany) *June 8, 2008*

253 Dr Ejaz Akram (Associate Professor (Religion and Politics),
 Humanities and Social Sciences, Lahore University of
 Management Sciences, Pakistan) *June 20, 2008*

254 Zainul Abidin Rasheed (Senior Minister of State for Foreign
 Affairs and Mayor of North-East District, Singapore) *June 21,
 2008*

255 Mr Ahmed Ali M. al-Mukhaini (Co-founder and Interfaith
 Activist, Christian-Muslim Majlis, Oman) *June 22, 2008*

256 Qaiser Shahzad (Lecturer and Research Associate, Philosophy
 and Science Unit, Islamic Research Institute, International
 Islamic University, Islamabad, Pakistan) *June 23, 2008*

257 Professor Dr. AbdelHaq Azzouzi (President of C.M.I.E.S.I,
 Morocco) *July 19, 2008*

258 Professor Salama Shaker (Deputy Foreign Minister of Egypt)
 July 22, 2008

259 Dr Mona Hassan (Assistant Professor of Islamic Studies,
 Departments of Religion and History, Duke University, USA)
 July 22, 2008

260 Dr Samir Kreidie (Chairman, Inma' Foundation, Managing
 Director, Rabya Trading and Agriculture Co Ltd) *July 29, 2008*

261 Ayatollah Prof. Dr. Ahmad Iravani (Director of Islamic
 Studies and Dialogue, Center for the Study of Culture and
 Values, Catholic University of America) *July 29, 2008*

262 Dr Sayyid Muhammad Syeed (National Director, Office
 of Interfaith and Community Alliance, Islamic Society of
 North America) July 29, 2008

263 Dr Mahmoud Ayoub (Faculty Associate in Shi'ite Islam and

Christian-Muslim Relations, Hartford Seminary, USA) *July 29, 2008*

264   Imam Suhaib Webb (American Islamic activist, speaker and religious scholar) *July 29, 2008*

265   Mr Shabbir Mansuri (Founding Director, The Institute of Religion and Civic Values (IRCV), USA), *July 29, 2008*

266   Shaykh Yasir Qadhi (Dean of Academic Affairs, AlMaghrib Institute, USA) *July 29, 2008*

267   Professor Dr Yahya Michot (Lecturer in Islamic Theology, Faculty of Theology, University of Oxford) *July 29, 2008*

268   Dr Hussam S. Timani (Professor of Religious Studies, Christopher Newport University, USA) *July 29, 2008*

269   Dr Syed Ali Wasif (President, Society for International Reforms and Research) *July 29, 2008*

270   Dr Noureddine Laftouhi (Professor, Cadi Ayyad University, Marrakech), *July 29, 2008*

271   Sara Shroff (Senior Director, Changing Our World, USA) July 29, 2008

272   Dr Fuad Nahdi (Director, Radical Middle Way, London) *August 13, 2008*

273   Shaikh Saleh bin Muhammad bin Hasan al-Asmari (Advisor, Ministry of Islamic Affairs, Director of the Institute for Sharia Studies, General Supervisor of the Manarat al-Sharia Network) *September 11, 2008*

274   Professor Abdul Ali Hamid (Principal, The Muslim College, London) *September 12, 2008*

275   Dr Ataullah Siddiqui (Director, Markfield Institute of Higher Education, Leicester) *September 12, 2008*

276   Dr Ahmed Mirza MD (Secretary, Naqshbandiya Foundation for Islamic Education, Phoenix, USA) *September 30, 2008*

277   Dr Özcan Hıdır (Dean of the Faculty of Islamic Sciences, The Islamic University of Rotterdam) October 6, 2008

278   Allama Abulfateh G R Chishti (President, Modern Islamic Studies Centre, Jamia Masjid Mai Saleem Akhtar New Sohan Capital District, Islamabad, Pakistan) *October 26, 2008*

279   Dr Abdalaziz Eddebbarh (Director of Ibn Ashir Institute of Islamic Studies, Imam of Taha Mosque, President of the Santa Fe Interfaith Leadership Alliance, USA) *October 28, 2008*

280   Habib Faisal El-Kef (Caller to Allah, Saudi Arabia) *October 30, 2008*

281   Dr Qamar-ul Huda (Senior Programme Officer, U.S. Institute

of Peace) *October 30, 2008*

282 Professor Ahmad Hianpiero Vincenzo (Johns Hopkins University in Bologna, President of the Society of Italian Muslim Intellectuals) *November 2, 2008*

283 Dr Sadiq Malki (Visiting Scholar, Center for Muslim-Christian Understanding, University of Georgetown, USA) *November 11, 2008*

284 Dr Yassin Ali al-Makusi (Professor at the World Islamic Sciences and Education University, Jordan) *November 20, 2008*

285 Engineer Marwan Awwad al-Fa'ouri (Secretary-General, International Moderation Assembly) *November 20, 2008*

286 Ms Aysha Nour Soulaq (Assistant, Justice and Development Party, Istanbul Municipality) *November 20, 2008*

287 Mr Amr al-Shobaki (Director of the United Arab European Studies Programme at Al-Ahram University) *November 20, 2008*

288 Shaykh Muhammad al-Hamddayi (President, Movement for Tawhid and Reform, Morocco) *November 20, 2008*

289 Mr Mehmet Zahid Gül (Writer and Researcher, Turkey) *November 20, 2008*

290 Mr Enver Yıgıl (Proprietor, Bahçesehir University, Turkey) *November 20, 2008*

291 Dr Bekir Karliga (Faculty of Arts, Galatasaray University, Turkey) November 20, 2008

292 Dr Abu Bakr Muhammad Ahmed Muhammad Ibrahim (Deputy Dean, Institute for the Islamization of Knowledge, Malaysia) *November 20, 2008*

293 Sheikh Tajuddin Hamid al-Hilali (Mufti of Australia) November 20, 2008

294 Dr Yousef al-Koudeh (President of the Sudanese Centre Party) *November 20, 2008*

295 Dr. Lakhdar Chreit (University of Algiers) *November 20, 2008*

296 Mr Muntasser al-Zayyat (Secretary-General of the Egyptian Bar Association) *November 20, 2008*

297 Prof. Muhammad al-'Aadil (President, the Turkish-Arabic Society, Ankara). *November 20, 2008*

298 Dr Sa'duddin al-Uthmani (Former Secretary-General in the Justice and Development Party, Morocco) *November 20, 2008*

299 Prof Dr. Azmi Taha al-Sayyid Ahmed (Editor-in-Chief, *Jordanian Journal for Islamic Studies*) *November 20, 2008*

300 Prof Dr Burhan Kuroglu (Professor, University of Bahçesehir, Director of the Centre for Civilization Studies) *November 20, 2008*

301 Imam Abu Eesa Niamatullah (Imam of the Cheadle Mosque, Cheshire, UK. Lecturer and Resident Scholar of the Cheadle Muslim Association) *January 12, 2009*

302 Khalid al-Anani (Senior Analyst, Expert on Political Islam and Democratization Middle East, Al-Ahram Foundation) *February 17, 2009*

303 Waleed El-Ansary (Assistant Professor of Islamic Studies, Department of Religious Studies, University of South Carolina, Columbia SC USA) *March 9, 2009*

304 Abdool Magid Abdool Karim Vakil (Founder and President of the Islamic Community of Lisbon (Communidate Islamica de Lisboa), Co-Founder and President of the Abrahamic Forum of Portugal (Forum Abraâmico de Portugal) and Member of the Committee for Religious Freedom, Ministry of Justice) *March 28, 2009*

305 Prof Dr Azzedine Gaci (President of the Regional Council of the Muslim Faith (CRCM, Lyon, France)

306 Sarah Joseph OBE (Editor *March 29, 2009* and CEO, *EMEL* Magazine, United Kingdom) *October 9, 2009*

307. Prof. Dr. Asma Afsaruddin, Professor of Islamic Studies, Indiana University at Bloomington, USA) *October 9, 2009*

CHRISTIANS AND MUSLIMS BREATHE A NEW SPIRIT

David Burrell, C.S.C.

Professor of Ethics and Development Studies,
Uganda Martyrs University, Nkozi
Hesburgh Professor Emeritus of Philosophy and
Theology, University of Notre Dame

ADDRESS TO THE CATHOLIC CHAPLAINCY
AT THE UNIVERSITY OF CAMBRIDGE

THE PAPACY CONTINUES to register symbolic valence, often more so for those who are not Catholic. A quick look at the acceleration of relations between Christians and Muslims within the scant two years since Regensburg contrasts dramatically with fourteen centuries of conflict or standoff. Many of us cannot help but attribute this dramatic turnabout to deep-flowing divine action in our current history: action starkly at variance with the prevailing Islamophobia in the west, evidenced in palpable fear in Europe and untutored prejudice in America. But let us first consider the unlikely chain of events since the professorial address at Regensburg, which the Pope used to develop a recondite thesis about the intrinsic role which reason has played in developing the Christian faith over the centuries. So far, a thoroughly Catholic view of the development of doctrine, with a sidelong critique of 'voluntarism' redolent of 'radical orthodoxy.' But it was the aside which offended, ostensibly offered in homage to Professor Khoury, who had been a colleague of professor Ratzinger at Regensburg. Not only does the aside offer contested views, but it is poorly constructed as well, with the lecturer quoting Khoury, who quotes the Byzantine Emperor Paleologus (shortly before the fall of Constantinople), to bolster a thesis about Islam's insouciance towards reason, itself bolstered by citation of an early work by the distinguished French Islamicist, Roger Arnaldez, on Ibn Hazm, proposing that Iberian 'hardline' thinker as the spokesperson for Islam. In short, so many citations within citations that the lecturer's view of the matters in question was utterly obfuscated. Careless rhetorical construction could not but lead to utter distraction, yet when an intelligent theologian who is also Pope distracts us, industrious speculators try to tell us what he meant by doing something so inept. So we were treated to inane western commentators suggesting what he must have intended, while 'friends of the court' invented astute reasons why a pope might have made such contentious statements—though we have seen that the concatenation of citations within citations makes it quite impossible to ascertain what the lecturer himself actually stated regarding the matters in question: the relevance of reason to Islam. So the most charitable comment would be that he made a gaffe, and the most salutary response of the Pope should have been to admit just that.

Yet within a month thirty-eight Muslim scholars took the initiative, reminding the lecturer of things he should have known, like medieval Christendom's reliance on

Islamic thinkers to develop their own doctrinal positions, notably on creation, and reminding readers of the polemical cast of both emperor Paleologus and Ibn Hazm. The official Vatican reaction was lukewarm, but the Pope himself offered a potent symbolic response on his visit to Istanbul, praying in a celebrated mosque. Yet other forces were at work, and a year after the initial Muslim response, a document appeared, endorsed by 138 Muslim thinkers, addressed to the Pope, the Archbishop of Canterbury, and other Christian leaders: *A Common Word*. Capitalizing on the Qur'anic statement, here rendered as 'a common word between us,' the document begins by reminding Christian leaders that Muslims and Christians make up more than half of the world's population, and proceeds to celebrate what we hold in common: *love of God and love of neighbour*. Freely citing from Christian and Muslim scriptures, the document challenges us all to reach for mutual understanding in the cause of peace. Scarcely a month later, the Yale Center for Faith and Culture, spearheaded by Miroslav Volf and Joseph Cummings, gathered 300 Christian signatories to a response printed as a full-page advertisement in the *New York Times* (18 November 2007). Five months later, the Vatican announced a Catholic-Muslim forum, to be jointly administered by five Muslim and five Catholic notables. Most recently, with the assistance of distinguished consultants, the Archbishop of Canterbury issued a theologically astute response on July 14, as the Yale Center for Faith and Culture convened a gathering of Christian and Muslim leaders, including a broad representation of the signatories to the *Common Word*, to probe the issue of love of God and neighbour in an explicitly comparative way. Moreover, the way the Yale conveners facilitated a broad evangelical representation in this gathering, as well as in the earlier published response, is perhaps most telling for America. In the face of Islamophobia in America and pervasive fear in Europe over the very presence of Muslims, deep counter-currents emerge: the Spirit must be at work!

In fact, the *Common Word* website lists more than fifty Christian responses, including an immediate response from the Vatican Secretary of State to Prince Ghazi bin Muhammad bin Talal of Jordan, conveying Pope Benedict's enthusiastic praise for the initiative, notably for its focus on love of God and neighbour. We have all been trained to be critical of texts, but it is more telling to note the nearly miraculous fact of garnering signatures of so many notables across a widely diverse Muslim world. It would appear that Prince Ghazi's pellucid Islamic culture pervades the *Common Word* initiative, from text to signatories. Let us try to ascertain what is at stake as well as what is actually taking place, as much as we can.

Meaning and truth; dialogue and proclamation

In encountering documents like the *Common Word*, we shall see how dialogue, like any probing conversation, attends to *meaning* rather than to *truth*. This should be evident enough, but attempts to contrast 'dialogue' starkly with 'proclamation' have obscured this simple point, by implying that dialogue is somehow deficient as a faith-strategy, since it stops short of proclaiming the truth. But what would it be to proclaim the truth? Would it be to make an assertion and then to insist that it was true; or as one wag put it: to stamp one's foot? In fact, of course, any properly formed assertion, actually stated, intends what is the case. Grammar is inherently ethical, which is why lying—deliberately stating what is not the case--is inherently wrong. Yet we know that our acceptance of what another says is often conditioned by the moral probity or veracity of the speaker. So 'proclaiming the truth' of one's faith is better done than said, as the Amish community in Pennsylvania demonstrated to America by forgiving their children's killer. Merely stating one's faith convictions cannot in fact count as proclamation. What counts is witness; and while the fact of dialogue may give telling witness in certain situations, like Israel/Palestine, the intellectual endeavour of dialogue can at best be a means of sorting out awkward from promising ways of stating what we believe. But this is hardly a deficiency; it is simply what any conversation tries to do. Authentic proclamation is quite another thing, as the gospels remind us again and again.

John Henry Newman, Bernard Lonergan, and Nicholas Lash can each be invoked as witnesses to this crucial distinction. Newman reminds us (in *Grammar of Assent*) how sinuous is the path to arriving at truth, and how delicate are the balancing judgments involved. Bernard Lonergan professedly acknowledges Newman's reflections when he parses Aquinas' insistence that truth can only be ascertained by way of judgment. And Nicholas Lash's recent *Theology for Pilgrims*[1] deftly exhibits the quality of dialectical reasoning which must attend reliable judgment. In the spirit of Wittgenstein, the witness Lash's writing gives to constructive and critical dialogue offers a healthy antidote to current TV confrontations which leave listeners to 'make up their own minds.' One can almost hear Wittgenstein query: 'I know how to make up my bed, but how might I make up my mind?' So whatever effective proclamation might be, it cannot be had without probing discussion and the conceptual

---

1 London: Darton, Longman and Todd, 2008.

clarification that dialogue can bring. Reduced to forthright assertion or downright insistence, it can neither be authentic nor effective. So there is no substitute for attending to meanings, as we attempt to minimize infelicitous expression in matters 'pertaining to God and the things of God' (as Aquinas views theology). For that same thinker reminds us that our language *at best* can but 'imperfectly signify God'.[2]

Yet precisely because of this slack which inevitably attends human language in speaking of the divine, thinkers operating within a tradition have often found space to interact with another tradition, so as to enrich their own. What we know as inter-religious dialogue has certainly been facilitated by the sea-change wrought by the Vatican II document, *Nostra Aetate*, but the practice of engaging one's own tradition by encounter with others has long been part of the creative assimilation of revelation which characterizes faith traditions. I have probed the ways Thomas Aquinas utilized the Jewish scholar, Moses Maimonides, as they both adapted the Islamic metaphysics of Avicenna, in an effort to offer a coherent account of free creation—a teaching shared among Jews, Christians, and Muslims in the face of formidable philosophical alternatives.[3] More recently, in the main narrative of Pope Benedict's Regensburg address, he delineated the sustained role which rational inquiry has played in the ongoing development of Christian revelation. For now, it will prove useful to propose the sophisticated ways in which medievals interwove faith with reason to develop a discipline we have come to know as theology, as a way of modeling interfaith exchange into an apt vehicle for developing doctrine. Recall Aquinas' simple recommendations: should

---

2 St Thomas Aquinas, *Summa Theologica*, 1.13.3.

3 David Burrell, *Freedom and Creation in Three Traditions* (Notre Dame: University of Notre Dame Press, 1993).

an apparent contradiction emerge between faith and reason, first determine whether the relevant interpretation of scripture is a faithful one, then look to see whether the reasoning in question has been carried out responsibly. To appreciate the new context, however, we shall have to expand John Paul II's discussion of 'faith and reason' (*Fides et ratio*) to embrace the variable of *culture*. For that encyclical explicitly notes how 'reason itself, in accord with which Christians experience their faith, is soaked in the culture of the place nearest to it, and in its turn ensures that with the progress of time, its own nature [i.e., what we take to be *reason* itself] is bit by bit transformed' (#71). Yet since that prescient reminder is never developed within the text itself, it remains our task to delineate how the cultural shift in interfaith attitudes augurs new theological potential.

Three neuralgic issues

Let us explore three neuralgic issues, beginning with that of 'trinity,' to illustrate how interfaith exchange can now offer an apt vehicle for developing doctrine. Christian-Muslim disputations regularly opposed Muslim insistence on the unicity of God to a Christian trinitarian presentation. Yet any student of the history of Christian thought knows how it took four to five centuries of Christological controversies, plus another century of conceptual elaboration, to hone a 'doctrine of trinity,' precisely because of the *shema*: 'Hear, O Israel, God our God is one' (Deut 6:6). If Muslim teaching showcasing divine unity—*tawhid*—has been developed polemically over against a misunderstanding of the 'threeness' of the one God, that should be perfectly understandable for Christians, given the time it took them to articulate 'threeness' in God without prejudice to

God's unity. Moreover, Islamic thought soon came to see how, as God's Word, the Qur'an must be co-eternal with God, lest God be mute![4] So once we emphasize the Johannine expression of 'word,' rather than the synoptic usage of 'son,' in dialogue with Muslims, we will at once be able to converse with them less polemically, yet also realize how thoroughly our baptismal formula refines the ordinary notion of *son*. And rather than diminishing the presentation of our faith, we will have come to a more refined understanding of what we have long been affirming. The fact remains that our faith is indeed 'trinitarian' while theirs is not, yet the process of dialogue will have brought us to a better articulation of our respective understandings of *trinity* and of *unity* in God.

The next example comes as a corollary to the intradivine relations, called (in common parlance) 'persons,' yet utterly different from the distinct individuals we normally identify as persons. We are speaking of the mediating role of Jesus in effecting our relationship to God. Muslims insist that while the Prophet delivers the Qur'an, which presents us with the very Word of God, it is our response to God's very Word which effects an immediate relation with God. Given the gift of the Qur'an, there can be no need for a 'mediator,' nor should one think of Muhammad as one. On the other hand, Christian scripture and theology speak in countless ways of Jesus Christ as 'mediator between God and human

---

4 For a succinct statement of the eternal Qur'an, see Kenneth Cragg's learned introduction to his *Readings in the Qur'an* (Portland OR: Sussex Academic Press, 1999): 'the Qur'an does not present itself as documenting what is other than itself. It is not about the truth; it is the truth ... as a book already existing eternally' (18); for an illuminating discussion, see Yahya Michot, 'Revelation,' in Tim Winter, ed., *Cambridge Companion to Classical Islamic Theology* (Cambridge: Cambridge University Press, 2008), p.185.

beings.' Now the ordinary use of 'between' makes it sound as though Jesus operates in a space between the creator and creatures. Yet that would be an Arian view, explicitly repudiated in the early councils, so in orthodox Christian belief Jesus' mediation operates theandrically; that is, as something intrinsic to Jesus' divine-human constitution, so carefully elaborated in early councils from Nicaea to Chalcedon. So while the actions of Jesus can effect an immediate relation to God as Father, Jesus does not mediate as a 'go-between.' So the very feature of mediation which Muslims deny to the Prophet, thinking that to be Jesus' manner of mediating, represents a distortion of Christian thought, though one in fact proposed by some Christians as well. One thinks of sixteenth-century debates between Protestants and Catholics, where the polemical edge doubtless distorted a more classical meaning of 'mediation.' For Catholics have elaborated a sense of 'mediator' to include ecclesial structures and personages, so that ordained persons 'mediate' the saving power of God to the faithful. But just as Jesus could not be construed, thanks to the *shema*, as a 'being alongside God' (which is the meaning Muslims attach to *shirk*: something--either created or uncreated--on a par with the creator), so Christians falsify their own faith if they conceive of Jesus' mediation (or, *a fortiori*, that of the church) as situated 'between' the creator and creatures. As the Word who is God, Jesus' mediation effects that immediate relation to God as Father which Christians presume in their recurrent prayer: 'Our Father'.

The final example explores the polemical stance both Jews and Muslims take with regard to Christian teaching regarding 'original sin.' Here again, applying Aquinas' hermeneutical cautions, we find that there are widely divergent versions of 'original sin' in diverse Christian lexicons, and one is never sure which one of them is at issue. The spectrum of meanings Christians attach to this teaching can be fairly represented between a characteristically Catholic view, captured in Chesterton's insistence that 'original sin is the only empirically verified Christian doctrine' (or 'Murphy's Law' in the moral order), to the most stark contention that its effects render our intellectual and voluntary faculties utterly dysfunctional. But these views all require that Adam's transgression somehow affect and infect us all by a path which remains obscure.[5] So they all focus on the universal human need for redemption, exemplified in and effected by Jesus' death on a cross. Now if this remains a sticking point for Muslims, an adequate way of articulating 'the atonement' continues to elude Christian theology, which deems Anselm's account deficient on several counts, but has yet to find a satisfactory formulation (though I find an illuminating one in Sebastian Moore's *The Crucified is no Stranger*[6]). Yet we can all recognize how incapable are rational creatures of achieving their inbuilt goal of union with God, so some action on the creator's part must make that possible— recalling Chesterton. Now a closer look at the Muslim view of human beings' capacity for 'drawing near to' God shows less difference between us than first appeared. Islamic thought takes the situation in the Hejaz before the Prophet's preaching the Qur'an, and readily applies it to the entire world: bereft of divine revelation, human beings are bound to wonder aimlessly, seeking to fulfill their own desires and inevitably engaging in deadly combat, as we see every day!

5 See Rudi teVelde's delineation of Aquinas' attempts in Rik Van Nieuwenhove and Joseph Wawrykow (eds.), *Theology of Thomas Aquinas* (Notre Dame IN: University of Notre Dame Press, 2005).
6 London: Darton, Longman and Todd, 1977.

On this view, the Torah or the 'Injil' (gospel, i.e. New Testament) serves the purpose for Jews or Christians that the Qur'an does for Muslims, since human beings left to themselves would never make it. So while Christianity focuses on the death and resurrection of Jesus, Muslims locate the redemptive act *par excellence* in the unmerited and serendipitous 'coming down' of the Qur'an from God through the Prophet. Human beings are invited to respond to this gift, and their everlasting redemption depends on the quality of that response. So this dynamic reinforces the fundamental analogy between Jesus and the Qur'an: as Christians believe Jesus to be the Word of God made human, Muslims believe the Qur'an to be the word of God made book. Each of these examples can show us how comparative inquiry will inevitably highlight dimensions of our own theological task, by accentuating items in our own traditions which need clarification and development.

How the examples culminate in an exposition of theological grammar

Moving beyond examples to the grammar proper to theology, we can note the 'play' of theological inquiry, rooted as it must be in practice, to display Aquinas' contention that our language, at best, will 'imperfectly signify' divinity (ST 1.13.3). And if theological expression will ever be inadequate, theological inquiry will ever be comparative, always seeking the least misleading modes of expression. Yet that requires refinement of judgment, gained by weighing different expressions relative to each other, in an effort better to articulate what Augustine called 'the rule of faith.' Yet if there can be no adequate expression, we shall always be weighing candidates relative to each other. And once the idol of 'pure reason' has been shattered, and we can learn to accept diverse ways of arriving at conclusions, we will also find that we can employ the skills learned in one tradition to follow reasoning in another. Traditions, in other words, are often found to be *relative to* one another in ways that can prove mutually fruitful rather than isolating. The traditions which prove to be so will be those which avail themselves of human reason in their development, as the patterns of stress and strain in their evolution will display their capacity for exploiting the resources of reason. (On this point, Pope Benedict was 'spot on,' as the 38 Muslim scholars noted, yet for both Muslim and Christian traditions!) In short, fears about 'relativ*ism*' give way to the human fact that all inquiry takes place within a tradition. So just as medieval ways of resolving apparent conflicts between faith and reason turned on critical hermeneutics with regard to texts, together with critical assessment of the reasoning one is employing, so interfaith comparative inquiry will require skills of reading one set of texts in relation to another.

So where have we come? To an interim conclusion, using the skills we have developed to subvert the perfectly normal desire of each religious group to show it is superior to all comers, even though characteristic efforts to do so will invariably involve presenting the other in ways which can at best be contested for fairness, and at worst display brutal colonization. A final charitable look at the 2000 Vatican statement *Dominus Iesus,* 'on the unicity and salvific universality of Jesus Christ and the Church,' can suggest a way of putting things less contentiously than that document did.[7] It purports merely to proclaim abiding Christian

---

7 See *Sic et Non: Encountering 'Dominus Iesus'*, edited by Stephen J. Pope and Charles Hefling (Maryknoll: Orbis, 2002).

truth, yet recalling our earlier discussion of 'proclaiming truth,' Article Two of the document effectively derails that intent. After expressing the elements of Christian faith in the words of the Nicene Creed in Article One, the authors go on to claim, with disarming self-assurance, that 'in the course of the centuries, the Church has proclaimed and witnessed with fidelity to the Gospel of Jesus.' Proclaimed, yes; but witnessed with fidelity? If this were true, past centuries would have been radically different and our own century surely unrecognizable. Indeed, a contestable assertion can fault an entire document. Nor is this a minor flaw, for this claim to have witnessed faithfully throughout the centuries, so out of touch not only with history but also with present day reality, can only make our proclamations arrogant and monopolistic. Indeed, ethical humility and intellectual humility are intimately related, as proclamation is to witness, as we have seen in the Amish example

So Christian theology must always begin, as does Christian worship, with a *mea culpa* and a *Kyrie eleison*. Its focus is proclamation, yet substantial moral failures of the Christian community will inevitably mute the truth claims we may make, as Pope Benedict has acknowledged in asking forgiveness for clerical abuse. Had the Christian community, including its officials, offered better witness to Jesus, claims about the role of the Church in God's saving plan and activity could find a more receptive audience.[8] Yet our discussion of the effects of interfaith dialogue, in this case with Muslims, can offer an alternative way of expressing the distinctiveness of Christianity, and do so in a fashion

---

8 These words are adapted from Dan Madigan, S.J.'s reflections on a discussion in which we both participated at Tantur Ecumenical Institute (Jerusalem) in 2006, which, edited by James Heft, will be published by Oxford University Press.

which might be intelligible to others: that our revelation is in a person. Preceded by an appropriate *mea culpa* regarding our collective ability as 'Christians' to follow that same Jesus (as John Paul II did during Lent in the same year 2000), we can simply remind ourselves that Christians believe that Jesus is the Word of God made human, while Muslims believe that the Qur'an is the word of God made book. These parallel formulae express profound difference as well as structural similarity, and recalling them can advance ecumenical interests as well as our own self-understanding as Christians. So the practice of dialogue can serve to affect, for the better, our attempts at proclamation as well. As our own sense of who we are develops in the face of generous Muslim initiatives like the *Common Word*, we will come to appreciate how much we need one another to appreciate as well as give witness to what we have received from God.

HUMAN DIGNITY AND MUTUAL RESPECT

Abdal Hakim Murad

Dean, the Cambridge Muslim College

ADDRESS TO THE FIRST CATHOLIC-MUSLIM FORUM,
ROME, 5 NOVEMBER 2008

YOUR EMINENCES, EXCELLENCIES, distinguished guests and friends. Peace be with you, and the mercy and compassion of God.

Our meeting in this historic place is, God willing, a celebration and a sign of hope. Celebration as we together feast on God's revealed words, nourished and sustained to carry the message of truth and reconciliation to the communities which we represent. And hope, in the assurance that the scrutiny which Heaven assuredly directs to our deliberations and to the states of our hearts in these days will overlook our many shortcomings, and be the sign under which the best and most fruitful exchanges of our two faiths in the past will continue to inspire us, while we find new and successful means of overcoming both those misunderstandings and those errors of intention which have, in past ages, led us into conflicts displeasing to God.

It is evident to us all how close is the relationship between the great subject of our discussions yesterday[1] and the subject which we address today. Indeed, it is this relationship which lies at the heart of the distinctiveness of the religious response to the crisis of modernity. Ours is an age in which noble efforts are made to esteem humanity, through codes of human rights and international conventions of many kinds. Yet the philosophy which, in today's prevailing secular climate, seeks to offer foundations to these efforts today seems to exist in a state of crisis. The Enlightenment, source of much that is precious to our contemporary understanding of human dignity, was attacked in its day by religious and also some secular thinkers who doubted the claims of a purely secular ethic, and of a categoric imperative rooted in an immense optimism about the moral capacity of unaided reason and science. That pessimism has, in part, proved reasonable. Europe, cradle of Enlightenment, is today the cradle of a postmodern relativism of a most virulent kind. The spirits released from the Pandora's box of the *Lumières* and the *Aufklärung*, and in my own country by Locke and Hume, have proven, in some cases, to be allies to the angels; but in others to be unmistakeably from the infernal realms of subversion and enmity. Europe – and I speak here as a European – is in crisis, and believers, who for so long, sometimes rightly, and sometimes cravenly, stood against the Enlightenment project, are called upon today to heal its deep pain. Christians and Muslims, as followers of Europe's two largest religions, must surely work together as never before in finding a remedy. We must also work to ensure that Europe's heart-sickness, expressed today in an

---

1 It was agreed that Day One of the Forum would be dedicated to the subject of 'Love of God and Love of Neighbour'.

almost unrivalled religious indifference, is not exported to the world.

This is, in fact, where I wish to direct my remarks. As a citizen and advocate of the European Union, I find myself part of a tragically Godless society. Recently a sociologist published a book with the title *The Death of Christian Britain*,[2] and this hurts me deeply, because in fact what is dying is a set of monotheistic convictions and a life of prayer and human giving that as Muslims we wish to see thrive around us. Yet I am also a member of Islam. That combination of the European and the Islamic is one that would be less difficult were Europe to be more faithful to the Christian dimension of its heritage. I prefer to live in a Christian society than in a secular one.

This sense of loss motivates my own particular commitment to the *Common Word* process. As you are aware, the meeting of this Forum here in Rome is one consequence of the initiative launched a year ago by Muslim scholars who, distressed by the current state of the world, offered a hand of support and goodwill to the spiritual heads of Christendom. My own reason for signing, in addition to the consensus of the document's signatories that the world is in need of healing, and that Muslims are summoned to call mankind to the undying principles of love of God and of neighbour, was that I am particularly distraught by Europe's lack of faith, and the diminution of human dignity and conviviality that surely results.

If, in many inner city areas, and increasingly elsewhere, Muslims live as a significant European constituency, then there is much scope for working together against our continent's current degraded view of human vocation and

---

2 Callum G. Brown, *The Death of Christian Britain* (London: Routledge, 2001).

destiny. And it is my belief that the Holy See's current insistence on the revival of the heritage of religious reason is entirely correct. It is important to recollect that the Catholic Church, as the world's oldest institution, has a long memory which encompasses other, earlier episodes when the prospects seemed dark. St Benedict of Nursia, fifteen hundred years ago, lived during barbarian invasions, which seemed to threaten Europe with a polytheistic relativism, and an inhuman ethic of greed and domination. The remedy, as Benedict saw, and as he lived in the actuality of his life, was the immense power of revealed certainty defended and reinforced by reason.

With its present leadership, the Holy See is well-placed to justify its claims to be a support for true reason. And this places it, as Muslims see matters, in an ideal position for cooperation with Muslims, and surely with others, in the great task of defeating pessimism and the rule of arbitrary opinion.

Islamic theology, we now know, took some of its early methods and categories from Christians such as John Philoponus, whom we knew as Yahya al-Nahwi.[3] Likewise, at key junctures in its own history, Christian Europe has been strengthened by the study of Islamic thinkers. Who can deny the impact of Ibn Rushd, the Shari'a judge of Cordoba, on Europe in the age of St Thomas Aquinas? Or the importance of Ghazali, known to the Latins as Algazel, in his rigorous refutation of the misplaced and sometimes sub-Pagan metaphysics of Avicenna? Or the *mutakallimun*, the Muslim theologians known as 'Loquentes' in the West, whose rigour in the use of reason made them ideal interlocutors, albeit at the distance required by the culture

---

3 Peter Adamson, 'Al-Kindi and the Mu'tazila: Divine Attributes, Creation and Freedom,' *Arabic Sciences and Philosophy* 13 (2003), 45-77.

of the time, for the most rigorous of Christian thinkers?[4] As Europe today confronts the new barbarians, who are the postmoderns and other relativists who, not from abroad, are from an evolution of its own inner life, such a convergence can prove a vital asset. Our mutual respect can be based on the practice of shared rational confrontation of Europe's disease.

The need to base our dialogue on ideas is further underlined by the imperative of mission, so salient in both traditions. A mere collaboration on practicalities would risk muffling the theological conversation which is surely close to the heart of any true comparison of the religions' claims.

Of the great European students of Islam in the past century, many of the greatest were faithful Catholics who, following Maritain and the neo-Thomist interest in Arabic philosophy, made profound contributions to our understanding of Muslim theology. Among them we must cite the great Dominican scholars, Georges Anawati and Louis Gardet, whose 1948 manual of Islamic theology shows the importance of reason to Islamic culture, and the value of detailed comparisons with Thomism.[5] Their Islamic focus was on Hanbalism and Ash'arism. But Maturidism, the third great school of Sunni theology, became the special concern of Josef Van Ess of Tübingen University. Van Ess has reminded us of the Maturidi insistence, present also in Ghazali and his school, on the rationality of God. In his

---

4 C.E. Butterworth and B.A. Kessel (eds.), *The Introduction of Arabic Philosophy into Europe* (Leiden: E.J.W. Brill, 1994); H.A. Wolfson, 'The Twice-Revealed Averroes', *Speculum* 36 (1961), 373-92; Jean Jolivet, 'The Arabic Inheritance', in Peter Dronke (ed.), *A History of Twelfth-Century Western Philosophy* (Cambridge: Cambridge University Press, 1988), pp.113-47.

5 Louis Gardet and M.-M. Anawati, *Introduction à la théologie musulmane: essai de théologie comparée* (Paris: J. Vrin, 1948).

great four-volume history of early Muslim theology, Van Ess stresses Islam's insistence on the divine ground of reason again and again. He even writes this:

> Christianity speaks of the "mysteries" of faith; Islam has nothing like that. For Saint Paul, reason belongs to the realm of the "flesh", for Muslims, reason, '*aql*, has always been the chief faculty granted human beings by God.[6]

Van Ess, and earlier Catholic scholars, have done the world an incalculable service. Secular activists of an earlier generation liked to see Islam as the worshipper of a God of unreason, a legalistic tyrant far removed from human analogy or concern. Often Islam was paired with Judaism, which an older Orientalism chose to see as analogously 'Semitic' in its rejection of Hellenic or any other type of reason. Here, for instance, is Ernest Rénan, the arch-rationalist, writing in 1862:

> At the present time, the essential precondition for the spread of European civilization is the destruction of the Semitic thing *par excellence* ... the destruction of Islam ... Islam is the most complete negation of Europe: Islam is fanaticism ... The future, sirs, is therefore Europe's, and Europe's alone ... Here is eternal war, the war which will end only when the last son of Ishmael dies in misery, or is banished through terror to the depths of the desert.[7]

Rénan, hero of the *lumières*, is convinced that Islam and Judaism can have nothing to say to the idea of human

---

6 Josef Van Ess, *The Flowering of Muslim Theology* (Cambridge MA: Harvard University Press, 2006), pp.153-4.

7 Ernest Rénan, *De la part des peuples sémitiques dans l'histoire de la civilisation*, discours d'ouverture du cours de langue hébraique, chaldaïque et syriaque au College de France (Paris: Michel Lévy, 1862), pp.27-8.

dignity. We would add that his understanding of classical Christianity is, of course, hardly more sympathetic.

By the grace of God, we have since moved on, and Muslims need to thank Catholic scholars for having banished older and effectively anti-Semitic categories in favour of an understanding of Islam as a faith in which reasoned belief in a reasonable God is central to serious theology.

Such Catholic scholars have allowed us an image of Islam which converges in key respects with modern Catholic understandings of the inherent dignity of human beings. Shaykh al-Buti has frequently referred to many of the Koranic indicants of this principle. 'We have ennobled the descendents of Adam', says the Koran (17:70). Adam alone is the creature to which God orders the angels themselves to bow down (7:11). This is because God has created within him a spirit which is from God Himself (15:29; 32:9; 38:72).[8] It is thus that our theorists, and particularly the Maturidis and Hanafis, insist that rights are innate in human beings, rather than conferred subsequently in a way that would make them entirely subject to religious confession. I would like to quote, in this connection, the words of Imam Sarakhsi, the Hanafi jurist who died in 1090:

> Upon creating human beings, God graciously bestowed upon them intelligence and the capability to carry responsibilities and rights. This was to make them ready for duties and rights determined by God. Then He granted them the right to inviolability, freedom, and property to let them continue their lives so that they can perform the duties they have shouldered. Then these rights to carry responsibility and enjoy rights, freedom, and property exist with a human being when he is born. The insane/

---

8 Muhammad Sa'id Ramadan al-Buti, *Man huwa sayyid al-qadar fi hayat al-insan* (Damascus, 1975).

child and the sane/adult are the same concerning these rights. This is how the proper personhood is given to him when he is born for God to charge him with the rights and duties when he is born. In this regard, the insane/child and sane/adult are equal.[9]

This high regard for the dignity of the human person, in medieval times produced societies where non-Muslim communities flourished for centuries. Naturally the assurance was that certain rights inhered more fully in those who accepted the final revelation of God in the Koran. That assurance was in no way strange for its time, and indeed may be regarded as normative in a certain way of traditional religion. Remember, much more recently, Pope Leo XIII, author of the encyclical *Libertas*, a theologically brilliant meditation on the nature of human dignity. This is his teaching:

> Justice therefore forbids, and reason itself forbids, the State to be godless; or to adopt a line of action which would end in godlessness – namely, to treat the various religions (as they call them) alike, and to bestow upon them promiscuously equal rights and privileges.[10]

Muslims, historically, would agree with this teaching. Some continue to do so today. But just as Papal teaching, even on matters of such grave moment, must and does change, so too Muslims must today, as a matter of some urgency, address their own failures in charity towards members of

---

9 Cited in Recep Sentürk, 'Minority Rights in Islam: From Dhimmi to Citizen', in Shireeen T. Hunter and Huma Malik (eds.), *Islam and Human Rights:Advancing a US-Muslim Dialogue* (Washington DC: Center for International and Strategic Studies, 2005, 67-99, p.74.

10 Pope Leo XIII, *Libertas*, 21.

minority religions.[11] But – and here we enter less familiar ground - Muslims are also called, by the same great teaching of the inalienable dignity of man, to press their various governments to respect the rights of Muslims as well. In too many Muslim countries the right of Muslims fully to practice the faith, to wear the garments decreed by tradition in public and educational places, to construct mosques and colleges, and to call freely for the reform of rulers they consider corrupt, is curtailed. Muslims must also, as well as calling for such necessary restorations of the Koranic ideal of the dignity and honour of the Adamic creature in countries where they form a majority, stand in solidarity with Muslims who live in parts of Europe where the rise of a new pagan tribalism is making life for the Muslim faithful intolerable. We know, and receive with respect and gratitude, the commitment of Catholic clergy and faithful, to overcome the many disadvantages faced by Muslim believers in Europe, most particularly in municipalities which are controlled by far-right political formations.

I have returned, as is evident, to my theme of the tragedy of Europe. I have already indicated my belief that, as supporters of the People of the Book, we lament Europe's spiritual crisis, and wish the Churches well in their struggle to heal it. I call to mind the writing of the Catholic conscience of Belgium, Jacques Neirynck. In his novel *The Siege of Brussels (Le siège de Bruxelles)*, Neirynck depicts a nightmarish future in which chauvinism has brought about the persecution and expulsion of Belgium's hated Muslim minority; but he closes by showing how the humane mainstream voices in Islam and Christianity will ultimately prevail.[12]

---

11 Abdal Hakim Murad, *Qur'anic truth and the meaning of* dhimma (Dubai: Kalam Research and Media, 2010).

12 Jacques Neirynck, *Le siège de Bruxelles, roman* (Brussels: Editions Labor, 2005).

My own confidence is that cooperation and mutual respect will, indeed, triumph against barbarism.

I turn now to an internal Muslim argument. Some Muslims appear to believe that this convivial, moral interaction and mutual support on issues of social concern must be detached from an attention to theology. In some cases one even hears the thought that Christianity, rooted in a belief in human sinfulness, is mistrustful of the intellect, and that its doctrines are based in a mere leap of faith. This is then contrasted with Islam which, such thinkers aver, is pre-eminently the religion of reason and of a reasonable God. One finds such perceptions in the polemics of Rashid Rida and his still very considerable school.[13] One hears it also among less cultivated Muslims. But it is clear from any study of Catholic doctrine that natural reason is central to the Catholic intellectual enterprise. This surely means that the claim that our cooperation should be merely pragmatic, not principial, is gravely misguided. It is time that Muslims welcomed cooperation with Catholics in an awareness that Catholicism, like Islam, speaks the universal language of reason.

Once this is achieved, there is much more to be achieved. Together, Muslims and Catholic Christians account for over two and a half billion souls: considerably over a third of the planet's population. The *Common Word* document stresses, from its scriptural perspective, the need not only to affirm the shared abstract principles of love of God and of neighbour, but to show the sincerity of our commitment in pastoral action. The two principles are in fact symbiotic.

We know that ours is a time of challenges to our relationship. There are Muslims, and there are Christians,

---

13 Rashid Rida, *al-Wahy al-Muhammadi* (Cairo: al-Manar, AH 1352), p. 195.

who wish that our gathering here had not taken place. The *Common Word* has been condemned by some Muslim voices; and some Christians have expressed their alienation from the warm and positive Christian responses which have come from Yale, Lambeth Palace, and other centres of the Christian conscience. In some places our relationship is improving; in others it seems to be suffering from an intractable deficiency. The commandment to love God and love neighbour, which is in practice a single commandment, is not always obeyed in practice and in our hearts. There is a valid Christian fear of Muslim extremism. And there is undeniably a Muslim fear of what Hans Küng, in his book on Islam, calls America's 'aggressive imperialistic foreign policy',[14] driven, as some see it, by Christian nationalists among whom, as he says, 'the crusade mentality is currently being revived.'[15] We both need to acknowledge the Other's fear of us.

As Muslims, called to be open-hearted towards the founders of all three Abrahamic faiths, we are particularly pained by such tensions. The *Common Word* initiative is one expression of that pain. But we must move forward. And one admirable advocate of this has been His Eminence Cardinal Tauran, in his message for the end of Ramadan, issued six weeks ago. He entitles his letter: *Christians and Muslims: together for the dignity of the family*. Here the cardinal commends past solidarity among Muslims and Catholics in the great task of defending this elemental institution of society, and prays for further collaboration in the future.

I believe that His Eminence is entirely correct, and that he has identified one of the most important areas in which our shared commitment to human dignity can find

---

14 Hans Küng, *Islam* (Oxford: Oneworld, 2007), p.453.
15 Küng, p.311.

practical expression. Muslims and Catholics alike, to the scorn of secular commentators, courageously uphold an image of marriage as the proper context for the expression of human sexuality. His Holiness Pope Benedict, in his encyclical *Deus Caritas Est*, has in a timely fashion reminded the world of the dignity and holiness of human sexual desire. The erotic should be part of our spirituality, not an alternative to it. The due context for this vital aspect of our dignity as incarnated beings is manifestly matrimony. And here, Muslims and Catholics will wish to differ from a certain reductionist tendency in contemporary culture to assume that men and women are different in ways that are only socially conditioned, rather than alternate, but equally valuable, expressions of aspects of the power of the One who has created humanity in the image of the Divine.

Let us borrow, in an analogising way, an insight from the Trinitarian theology of Hans Urs von Balthasar. Here the Swiss genius-theologian draws our attention to the relationship between the persons of the Trinity. He writes: 'The hypostatic modes of being constitute for each other the greatest opposition we could think of [...] precisely so that the most intimate interpenetration we could think of becomes possible.'[16] And, defying the impoverished modern view of gender, he goes on to identify the giving and taking of the persons of the Trinity in frankly gendered terms: the masculine principle identified with the fecundating, dynamic role, and the feminine with the receptive and the florescent.[17] Such a validation of classical

---

16 Hans Urs von Balthasar, *Theo-drama* II, 258, cited in Rowan Williams, 'Balthasar and the Trinity', 37-50 of Edward T. Oakes SJ and David Moss (eds), *The Cambridge Companion to Hans Urs von Balthasar* (Cambridge, 2004), see p. 41.

17 *Theo-drama* V, cited in Rowan Williams, 'Balthasar and the Trinity', p.45.

Christian understandings of the mutuality of the genders in family life is clearly close, in its outcomes, to Muslim assurances; although the Trinitarian language about the inner life of God is undeniably far from Islamic faith. Shared conclusions about the value of 'alternative sexualities' will surely follow.

Another area where we have already worked together to good effect is indicated in Archbishop Rowan William's splendid and detailed response to the *Common Word*.[18] He points to the importance of the Israeli-Palestinian conflict, as 'at or near the top of the list of issues that concern both Christians and Muslims all over the world'. Muslims are convinced that the Apostolic See, concerned for the Catholic and other communities of Jerusalem, will stand in solidarity with Christian and Muslim believers who, while renouncing cruel and arbitrary terroristic responses, stand courageously for their right to dignity in their own land. Muslims have been immensely heartened by the courage of many Christians, such as former American president Jimmy Carter, and Archbishop Desmond Tutu of Cape Town, in condemning what they describe as Israel's 'apartheid' policies against the Muslim and Christian communities of the occupied territories. It has been rightly said that upholding the dignity of the Palestinian people is the surest path to Muslim hearts, and we are confident that the Vatican will remember this as it attempt to advocate a peaceful and just solution for Jews, Muslims and Christians alike in the Holy Land.

But there are other places in God's earth where human dignity is being outraged. It is not right for Muslims, including Arab Muslims, to call attention to the plight of

---

18 Rowan Williams, 'A Common Word for the Common Good' (www. archbishopofcanterbury.org/1892).

the Palestinians, and to pay less attention to the victims of the current atrocities in Darfur. That scandal needs to be urgently explained and addressed. And even more recently, the tragedy in Eastern Zaire is summoning us all to joint action. One recalls, with reassurance, the good relations which were so frequently maintained between Catholics and Muslims in neighbouring Rwanda, even at the height of the appalling events of the early 1990s.[19]

Such calamities which disfigure God's earth are a summons, and a judgement. We have not always been agents of God's peace. It is surely a source of discomfort for us to learn that the twentieth century's most celebrated man of peace, Gandhi, was neither a Muslim nor a Christian. And as a European, citizen of a continent which is proud of its monotheistic heritage, I continue to be desolated by the memory of the wars of the past century, which outstripped both in scale and ferocity those of any other continent.

We are called, it is evident, to prove to the world that we are a force for good. The modern crisis of faith is all too often triggered by a sense that religion yields the bitter fruit of enmity and even conflict. Our most urgent task, then, as we seek to recover our place as defenders of human dignity and mutual respect, is to show, in practice, and not only in words, that we can cooperate together for the common good. Natural disasters, seemingly so prominent in our environmentally troubled times, offer an obvious field for common labour, and one follows with delight the progress of the cooperation between CAFOD and Islamic Relief, after the historic Memorandum of Understanding which they signed in 2003, in which they pledge support for each

---

19 Anne Kubai, 'Walking a Tightrope: Christians and Muslims in Post-Genocide Rwanda', *Islam and Christian-Muslim Relations*, 18 (2007), pp.228-34.

other's activities in emergency work.[20] Islamic Relief and Christian Aid are also, in my own country, sending joint Muslim-Christian teams to areas of southern Africa, in a pilot scheme which holds the promise of further and more systematic cooperation. And at the enormous Cut the Carbon Rally in Birmingham, on August 21, 2007, Christian Aid, and several Muslim charities, demonstrated the healing power of a public event which announces to the world that its environmental suffering can be healed by interreligious cooperation, pooling energy and resources to tackle a problem that is too large for the agencies of one faith alone.

The global famine that seems to come ever closer, prompted, perhaps, by the rise in biofuel consumption, is already creating lethal competition for scarce resources in many Third World countries. Deaths from hunger are increasingly reported, and small producers too are suffering. In India, figures show that an appalling 166,000 farmers have committed suicide since 1997.[21] Our shared wisdom regarding just distribution, compassion for the needy, the evils of usury, and a political struggle on behalf of the oppressed, should surely be put to use in a joint campaign, in the name of our father Abraham, to defend those who suffer in this way.

This should be particularly our duty and burden. Both Islam and Catholicism are in Europe. But neither should claim a privileged relationship with that continent, for fear of relegating others to a secondary status. Both of our traditions have substantial roots in Asia and Africa. Asia is, in one sense, the privileged continent, the continent of the spirit, as Heaven has made it the birthplace of all the major religions. Today many parts of it thrive, but in others, hu-

---

20 www.cafod.org.uk/partnership/other-faiths
21 Randeep Ramesh, *The Guardian*, 1 March 2008.

man dignity is suffering grievously. And in Africa, now a continent shared intimately between Islam and Christianity, we are also called to work together for what we hold in common. Jesus and Muhammad were not only champions of the poor, they lived among the poor, and will surely be resurrected among them. That is a vital aspect of their brotherhood and of ours. If we live in privilege, taking vain pride in our titles and garments, but fail to work with our own hands and hearts for those whose livelihoods are precarious, then we will have betrayed the Abrahamic principle of submission to God's will, which is that we be ready to sacrifice even what is most precious to us, unhesitatingly, with full hearts for God's sake.

The words of the Koran are summoning and reproaching us all:

> *Have you seen the one who denies religion?*
> *It is he who pushes away the orphan,*
> *And who does not urge the feeding of the poor.*
> *So woe to those who worship,*
> *Who are absent-minded in their prayer;*
> *Those who make a show of themselves,*
> *And refuse neighbourly assistance.*

(Sura 107)

SUGGESTIONS FOR FURTHER READING

LEARNING ABOUT CHRISTIANITY

The Cambridge Annotated Study Bible: New Revised Standard Version.
   Notes and References by Howard Clark Lee (Cambridge:
   Cambridge University Press, 1993).

Linda Woodhead, *Christianity: A Very Short Introduction* (Oxford:
   Oxford University Press, 2004).

Delbert Burkett, *An Introduction to the New Testament and the
   Origins of Christianity* (Cambridge: Cambridge University
   Press, 2002).

Joseph Ratzinger, *Introduction to Christianity* (San Francisco:
   Ignatius Press, 2004).

H. Bacovain (translator), *The Way of a Pilgrim: Spiritual Classics
   from Russia* (New York: Bantam Doubleday, 2000).

John Stott, *The Radical Disciple* (Nottingham: IVP 2010).

Rowan Williams, *Ponder These Things: Praying with Icons of the
   Virgin* (Norwich: Canterbury Press, 2002).

LEARNING ABOUT ISLAM

Muhammad Asad (text, translation and commentary), *The
   Message of the Qur'an* (Watsonville CA: The Book Foundation,
   2004).

Charles le Gai Eaton, Kabir Helminski and Mahmoud Mustafa
   (editors), *The Book of Hadith: Sayings of the Prophet Muhammad*
   (Watsonville CA: The Book Foundation, 2007).

Martin Lings, *Muhammad: His Life based on the Earliest Sources*
    (Cambridge: Islamic Texts Society/Allen and Unwin, 1983).
William Chittick and Sachiko Murata, *The Vision of Islam*
    (London: I.B. Tauris, 2000).
Shelinah Zahra Janmohamed, *Love in a Headscarf: A Muslim
    Woman seeks the One* (Aurum Press, 2009).
Sumbul Ali-Karamali, *The Muslim Next Door: The Qur'an, the
    Media and that Veil Thing* (Ashland, OR: Caveat Press, 2008).
Rusmir Mahmutcehajic, *On Love in the Muslim Tradition
    (Abrahamic Dialogues)* (Fordham: Fordham University Press,
    2007).

BOOKS ON DIALOGUE AND ENCOUNTER

Jack Goody, *Islam in Europe* (Cambridge: Polity, 2004).
Michael Ipgrave (editor), *Justice and Rights: Christian and Muslim
    perspectives* (Georgetown, Washington DC: Georgetown
    University Press, 2009).
C. David Lundberg, *What God Really Wants you to Know: God's
    Universal Truths Shared by All World Religions* (New Fairfield
    CT: Heavenlight Press, 2008).
Maria Rosa Menocal, *The Ornament of the World: How Muslims,
    Jews and Christians Created a Culture of Tolerance in Medieval
    Spain* (New York: Little, Brown and Company, 2003).
Norman Solomon, Richard Harries and Tim Winter (eds.),
    Abraham's Children: Jews, Christians and Muslims in Conversation
    (Edinburgh: T & T Clark/Continuum: London and New
    York, 2005).
Carl Vett, *Dervish Diary: Two Weeks in a Sufi Monastery in Istanbul*
    (Freiburg: Bridges Publications, 2007).
Mehnaz Heydarpoor, *Love in Christianity and Islam: A
    Contribution to Religious Ethics* (London: New City, 2002).
Miroslav Volf, Ghazi bin Muhammad and Melissa Yarrington
    (eds.), *A Common Word: Muslims and Christians on Loving God
    and Neighbour* (Grand Rapids: Eerdmans, 2010).
Waleed El-Ansary and David K Linnan (eds.), *Muslim and
    Christian Understanding: Theory and Application of 'A Common
    Word'* (New York: Palgrave Macmillan, 2010).

INTERNET RESOURCES

www.acommonword.com
www.interfaith.org.uk
cmcu.georgetown.edu
www.interfaith.cam.ac.uk
www.threefaithsforum.org.uk
www.transcendingjerusalem.com
stethelburgas.com
www.dialoguesociety.org

INDEX OF SCRIPTURAL CITATIONS

Holy Qur'an

Holy Bible

INDEX